ANCIENT GREECE

Niki Drosou-Panagiotou

PAPADIMAS
EKDOTIKI

Scientific editor: Panos Valavanis, Archaeologist, Professor of Archaeologiy
at the University of Athens

Reconstructions*: Georgios P. Antoniou, Architect-Engineer NTUA, MA UoYork

Photographs: Studio Kontos-Photostock, S. Mavrommatis, M. Pouliasis,
K. Kyriakidis, EFA, TAP

Publication editor : Evangelia Chyti

Translation: Alexandra Doumas

Creative modelling, Image-processing: Ledy Griva

CTP - Printing: NON STOP PRINTING L.T.D.

© copyright 2009 worldwide:
Dim. Papadimas Reg't Co., 56-58 Charilaou Trikoupi St, Athens 10680
Tel.: (++30) 210 3640235, 210 3645830
Fax: (++30) 210 3636001, e-mail: papa-ekd@otenet.gr

ISBN 978-960-6791-58-1

CONTENTS

PELLA ⊙

THESSALONIKI ⊙

VERGINA ⊙

DION ⊙

DODONA ⊙

DELPHI ⊙

ATHENS ⊙

CORINTH ⊙

OLYMPIA ⊙   MYCENAE ⊙   SOUNION ⊙

TIRYNS ⊙   AEGINA ⊙   DELOS ⊙

EPIDAUROS

RHODES ⊙

CRETE ⊙

INTRODUCTION

It is not known when man first appeared in the Greek Peninsula, but animal bones and Palaeolithic tools bear witness to his existence there in the Middle Palaeolithic (100,000-33,000 BP). About 40,000 years ago, a new type of man, Homo sapiens, who made stone tools by a new technique, emerged on the forestage of history, radically altering the course of mankind. The major climatic changes that took place around the ninth millennium BC, with the end of the Ice Age, had a dramatic effect on man's life and created the preconditions for the Neolithic Revolution. Thus, from the seventh millennium BC man became involved with agriculture and animal husbandry, and began to live in organized settlements, such as Nea Nikomedeia, Sesklo, Dimini and other sites in Greece.

Around 2800 BC, the use of metals, primarily bronze, was introduced in Greece. The land was now inhabited by Pelasgians, Carians and Lelegians (prehellenic tribes). Other tribes from Asia Minor settled on Crete and created the Minoan Civilization, the earliest civilization in Europe. In the islands of the Cyclades another distinct culture developed, known as Cycladic. Concurrently, the Helladic Culture flourished on the Greek Mainland.

The Achaeans, the Ionians and the Aeolians were the first Hellenic tribes of Indo-European origin to reach Greece around 2000 BC. They created the first truly Greek civilization, the Mycenaean (1580-1100 BC). Around 1400 BC, the Achaeans occupied Knossos, Rhodes and Cyprus, set up trading posts (emporia) in Asia Minor and developed commercial and diplomatic relations with the Egyptians, the Assyrians and the Hittites. They built palaces on hilltops fortified by Cyclopean walls and fostered all branches of the arts.

Another Hellenic tribe, the warlike Dorians, appeared in the late twelfth century BC. The "Coming of the Dorians" caused the collapse of the Mycenaean Civilization, with the resultant uprooting of large population groups from their ancestral hearths. The system of writing - Linear B script - was forgotten, artistic production declined and maritime trade ceased. This period is known as the "Dark Age" of Greece.

It was followed by the Geometric period (1100-700 BC), principal characteristic of which was the decoration of vases with geometric and linear motifs. Around the ninth century BC, the Greeks adopted from the Phoenicians the alphabet, from which the Latin and Cyrillic alphabets subsequently developed. A wave of colonization commenced around 800 BC, with the founding of Greek colonies in the Mediterranean and the Euxine Pontus (mod. Black Sea), accompanied by a burgeoning of the Arts and Letters. This was the age of the Homeric Epic.

The eighth century BC saw the birth of the city-states, such as Athens, Corinth, Megara, Argos, Thebes and others, which were no longer ruled by kings but by councils of aristocrats (oligarchies). The city-states grew into large and wealthy commercial and artistic centres. However, social conflicts and political upheavals brought the need for legislative reforms, such as those introduced by the law-givers Lykourgos in Sparta, Drakon and Solon in Athens. Despite the fragmentation into city-states and the rivalries between them, the Greeks were ever conscious of their ethnic unity, maintained through their common language, the institutions of the panhellenic games (Isthmian, Nemean, Olympian, Pythian), the panhellenic sanctuaries and the amphictyonies, that is, the assemblies of the representatives of the cities. In this period, which is known as Archaic, the Arts and Sciences flourished. The first monumental temples were built in the Doric and the Ionic order, large-scale sculpture appeared with the statues of kouroi and korai, as well as the black-figure and later the red-figure style in vase-painting. At the same time, philosophy was born.

In the mid-sixth century BC, a new threat loomed from Asia. King Cyrus captured Lydia, realm of Croesus, and subjugated many Greek cities of Asia Minor. These cities soon revolted and with the assistance of Athens struggled to cast off the Persian yoke. In 494 BC, Darius quashed the rebellion and launched a military campaign to punish Athens. In 490 BC, the Persians, with an army some 50,000 strong, reached the Plain of Marathon. The Athenians sought the help of the other Greek cities and prepared to confront the invaders. Under the leadership of General Miltiades, 11,000 soldiers (10,000 Athenians and 1,000 Plataiaians) won a decisive victory at Marathon, against all odds.

Ten years later, in 480 BC, Xerxes son of Darius launched a new expedition against Greece, with countless troops and 1,200 ships. He crossed the Hellespont (mod. Dardanelles), marched into Europe and descended upon Greece. At the defile of Thermopylai, Leonidas with 300 Spartans and 700 Thespians tried to stem this tide. But the Greeks fell to a man in this terrible battle. A monument at the site reminds visitors of their valiant sacrifice. The Persian army continued its course, destroying and plundering cities such as Thespiai and Plataiai, and eventually arrived at Athens. The city, the Acro-polis and the few Athenians who had remained were committed to the flames. The Greek armies withdrew to the Isthmus of Corinth, while their warships anchored close to the island of Salamis. There, under the command of the Athenian Admiral Themistokles, the united Greek fleet won a resounding victory, utterly devastating the Persian Navy in the famous Naval Battle of Salamis. One year later, in 479 BC, the combined Greek forces headed by General Pausanias, vanquished the Persians and slew their Commander-in-Chief Mardonius in the battle of Plataiai. Athens benefited most from these great and impressive victories.

In 477 BC the Athenians founded an alliance of 300 cities, centred on the sanctuary of Apollo on Delos and with a common treasury: the well-known "Delian League". Concurrently, the enormous task began of rebuilding the monuments on the Acropolis, which the Persians had razed to the ground. Thus was inaugurated the so-called "Golden Age" of Pericles, a most illustrious period in which Philosophy, History and Drama developed apace. Monuments of architecture and sculpture non pareil were erected on the Acropolis.

Although the two leading cities of Hellas, Athens and Sparta, drew up a peace treaty in 445 BC, this was short-lived. In 431 BC Greece was divided by civil strife, with the outbreak of the "Peloponnesian War", which spread to the whole land and lasted some 27 years. It ended in 404 BC with the defeat and surrender of Athens. The entire country was laid waste.

New conflicts arose between the Greek cities, in most of which victorious Sparta installed oligarchic regimes. But the days of Sparta's hegemony were numbered, as the other cities allied against her. Thebes emerged as protagonist in this historical phase. Two notable Theban politicians and soldiers, Pelopidas and Epameinondas, orchestrated the ignominious defeat of Sparta at Leuktra in Boeotia, in 371 BC, bringing Spartan sovereignty to an end and expanding Theban domination over virtually the whole of Greece. But the brief glory of Thebes died with these two men.

Shortly after, the King of Macedon, Philip II, came to the fore. A perspicacious statesman and an able diplomat, he had conceived the idea of uniting all the Greek cities into a single state. On the pretext of the Fourth Sacred War (339-338 BC), Philip intervened, punished the Amphissans and proceeded to Chaironeia (338 BC), where he crushed the Athenians and Thebans, who had joined forces against him. One year later, Philip convened a panhellenic council at Corinth, which established peace and alliance among all Greeks, and unanimously appointed the Macedonian king commander of the campaign against the Persians. In 336 BC, however, Philip - victim of a palace plot - was assassinated by one of his officers, Pausanias.

He was succeeded by his son Alexander, who though barely 20 years old promised to fulfill his father's ambitious plans. Alexander quickly suppressed insurrections of both Illyrian and Greek cities, convened another two panhellenic councils at Corinth and revived the Greek alliance. He then set forth for Asia, at the head of an army and navy against the Persians. Within a decade he vanquished the Persian army several times, became lord of Asia Minor, Syria, Palestine, Egypt, Sogdiane, and reached as far as the Indus Valley. Wherever he went, he founded cities, which were hearths of Hellenic civilization. But when Alexander died in 323 BC, at the age of 33, his vast empire was carved up between his generals into kingdoms. The period that followed is known as Hellenistic.

There were incessant wars between the successor kingdoms. In Greece two alliances of cities emerged, the Achaean Confederacy in the Peloponnese and the Aetolian Confederacy in Central Greece. Their purpose was to thwart the conquering designs of the Macedonians. Taking advantage of the civil conflicts, the Romans intervened in the internal affairs of the Greek cities. The Roman conquest of Greece was rapid. It started with the battle of Cynocephalae in 197 BC, in which Titus Quintus Flaminius defeated Philip V of Macedonia, continued with the defeat of King Perseus of Macedonia by Aemilius Paulus at Pydna in 168 BC, and was completed with the sack of Corinth by Lucius Mommius in 146 BC.

Greece now became a Roman province. During the period of Roman Rule, the country suffered many disasters, not least Athens, which was looted and its population decimated by Sulla in 86 BC. Nonetheless, the radiance of Greek Civilization had a significant influence on the Romans.

In the third and fourth centuries AD, Greece was subjected to new trials and tribulations, with the catastrophic incursions of the Barbarian hordes of Goths and Heruls. In AD 330, Emperor Constantine founded Constantinople, which essentially became capital of the entire province. Many important works of art were transferred there from all over Greece. A new age dawned.

ATHENS

Throughout the long history of Athens, its nucleus has always been the Acropolis and all important events took place upon or around this rock. The Pelasgians and the other Hellenic tribes, which tradition has it lived here prior to the arrival of the Ionians, around 2000 BC, fortified the Acropolis and gave the mountains and rivers of Attica their ancient names, which have remained in use to this day: Hymettos, Lykabettos, Ilissos, and so on.

In the prehistory of Athens, historical memories are interwoven with mythological elements. When Kekrops was king of the city he named it Kekropia and established the worship of Athena, goddess of wisdom, instead of Poseidon, god of the sea. The city then took the name of the goddess of wisdom, and has been known as Athens ever since. Kekrops' successors, Pandion, Erechtheus, Aegeus and Theseus, ruled wisely and contributed to the development of the realm. All of them dwelt in the palace on the Acropolis and some of them were buried there.

The legendary Theseus, who was lauded for many brave feats, freed Athens from the blood tribute she was obliged to pay to the Cretan king Minos, ruler of the seas, by slaying the Minotaur. He also succeeded in uniting the twelve demes of Attica under his sceptre and making Athens capital of the land. In memory of this event, the most splendid festival of Athens, the Panathenaia, was later instituted.

The last king of Athens was Kodros, who was said to have sacrificed his life heroically, in order to save the city from the Dorians. After his death, kingship was abolished and replaced by an elected aristocracy. However, this failed to resolve the differences between the wealthy landowners and the impecunious farmers.

So, political unrest continued until the sixth century BC, when the prudent Solon appeared on the scene. He introduced a new constitution, solving the problem of the poor men's debts to the rich. His legislation continued in force even when Peisistratos seized power (560-528/7 BC). Although his rule of the city was absolutist, as tyrant, he supported the poor and adorned the Acropolis with monuments. Henceforth the sacred rock was exclusively a place of worship.

The end of the tyranny came when one of Peisistratos' sons, Hipparchos, was assassinated by the tyrannicides Harmodios and Aristogeiton, sons of the noble Alkmeonid family. Another member of this family was the lawgiver Kleisthenes, who in 507/6 BC amended and supplemented Solon's legislation, founding the Athenian Democracy.

The Arch of Hadrian which separated the old city of Athens from the new

Bust of Pericles

After the major victories over the Persians, which are associated with the names of Miltiades and Themistokles, came the period of Kimon, which too was filled with great victories and achievements.

In 461 BC, Pericles was elected by the people and ruled Athens until his death in 429 BC. During his period the democratic regime was consolidated and the Arts and Letters, reached the pinnacle of their glory. But what made Pericles immortal was the building of the unsurpassed monuments on the Acropolis, in place of the earlier temples that had been destroyed by the Persians in 480 BC.

So important were the creations of this civilization that they withstood the test of time and the trials that beset the city: the Peloponnesian War, the destruction by the Roman general Sulla, who looted many treasures and dispatched them to Rome, and the invasion by the Heruls in AD 267. In the meantime, there had been a significant revival in the second century BC, due to the great admirer of the city of Athens, Emperor Hadrian, and its major benefactor, Herodes Atticus.

Until the sixth century AD, Athens was the cultural centre of the world, thanks to its illustrious past and to its renowned schools of rhetoric and philosophy, which were still thriving. However, in AD 529 Emperor Justinian closed down these schools and with them the glory of Athens waned. Over the years, Athens devolved into a provincial town, whose fate was the same as that of the rest of Greece.

After the centuries of Byzantium and of Ottoman rule, Athens was declared capital of the newly-founded Greek State in 1834. Almost immediately, works began on clearing and restoring the monuments on the Acropolis, in an effort to heal some of the wounds left by wars, fanatics and ignorance.

Reconstruction of the monuments on the sacred rock of the Acropolis, from the west →

THE ACROPOLIS

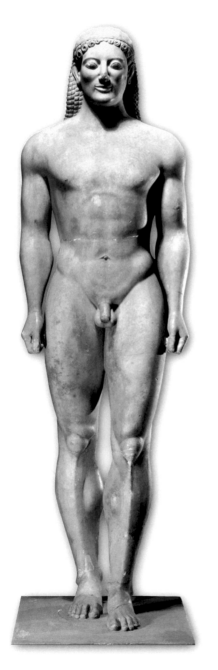

There are ancient ruins dispersed throughout Modern Athens, but at the heart of the city, as always, looms the Acropolis with its major sanctuaries and the cultural buildings on the south slope (theatre, odeum). Just beyond was the Agora, the hub of the city and the arena of the Athenian Democracy.

Some 500 metres west of the Acropolis stand three hills. The first was dedicated to the Muses, patrons of Sciences and the Arts, but is known today as Philopappus Hill, after the mausoleum built on top of it in the second century AD, by Gaius Iulius Antiochus Philopappus, a potentate from Syria who was an admirer and benefactor of Athens.

The second hill is the Pnyx, on which assembled the Ekklesia of the Deme, the cradle of democracy; there Athenian citizens gained the right to vote, for the first time in the history of mankind.

The third hill was dedicated to beauty, that is to the Nymphs. Closer to the foot of the Acropolis is the rocky hillock (Pagos) that was dedicated to the god Ares, the Areios Pagos or Areopagus.

According to Aeschylus' Oresteia, this was the birthplace of Justice, from the time when Orestes was tried here for murdering his mother Clytaemnestra and her paramour Aegisthus.

The Anavyssos Kouros

THE PROPYLAIA

The only route of access to the Acropolis was from its west slope, even in prehistoric times. It was from this side that Theseus entered to go to his palace, and Pericles too, when he took part in the procession of the Panathenaia. The Panathenaic Way, which started from the Kerameikos, wended its way up to the Propylaia There were no steps, just shallow transverse grooves to facilitate the ascent of men and of animals bringing materials for building the edifices or intended for sacrifices and rituals.

In Roman times a monumental staircase was built in front of the Propylaia, and later a gateway, known today as the Beulé Gate, after the French archaeologist Ernst Beulé, who discovered it in 1852, under the Ottoman bastion. Almost at the top of the ascent stands a rectangular pedestal, which was erected to hold the statue in honour of Eumenes II, King of Pergamon, but upon which in the Roman period the portrait statue of Marcus Vispanius Agrippa, son-in-law of Augustus and benefactor of Athens, was put up.

The Propylaia were 74 metres long, occupying the entire west side of the Acropolis. They are an imposing construction, worthy of the wonderful temples on the Sacred Rock.

The eminent architect Mnesikles, who was responsible for building the Propylaia, used mostly white Pentelic

The Varvakeion Athena, copy of the statue of Athena in the Parthenon

The Propylaia, detail of the east front

marble, with grey Eleusinian marble in places. Work began in 437 BC, but was cut short in 431 BC, due to the Peloponnesian War. Consequently, the lifting bosses on the marble blocks used for the external walls were not trimmed away.

The Propylaia comprised a central building (24 x 18.20 m.) and two wings, right and left. A marble cross-wall punctuated by five portals divides the central building into two façades, an east and a west, each fronted by six Doric columns and a pediment.

The central building is divided lengthwise into three parts by two rows of Ionic columns. The harmony and symmetry of this architectural masterpiece is obviously due to this combination of the Doric and Ionic orders.

The ceiling consisted of marble beams that rested on the walls and the Ionic columns, and of marble coffers. Traces of metal and painted stars, which were affixed to the coffers, allow us to reconstruct the strikingly attractive effect of the ceiling, which was like a blue sky spangled with golden stars.

The north wing was a spacious hall decorated with paintings by great artists, such as Polygnotos (5th c. BC), and was accordingly called the Pinakotheke ("picture gallery"). It was furnished with couches on which visitors could relax and was also used as a venue for official banquets of the city of Athens.

In Byzantine times the Propylaia became the seat of a bishop. For Franks and Florentines they served as a commandery or a residence, while the Ottoman Turks converted them into a gunpowder store.

Lightning struck the building in 1645 and the gunpowder ignited, causing irreparable damage to Mnesikles' magnificent creation.

Reconstruction of the Propylaia, the monumental entrance to the Sacred Rock →

THE TEMPLE OF ATHENA NIKE

The temple is built upon a tower, southwest of the Propylaia. The cult of Athena on this spot was very ancient, because from Mycenaean times the tower protected the gate of the Acropolis and perhaps served as a lookout post as far as the sea. Later, Nike (Victory) was identified with the goddess Athena. And because the wooden cult effigy (xoanon) of Athena, which represented her standing and holding a pomegranate in one hand, did not have wings - which were customary in representations of Nike - she was called Wingless Victory. It was subsequently said that the goddess had no need of wings, because she should never leave this place.

Building of the temple commenced in 421 BC, to designs by Kallikrates, who also took part in the construction of the Parthenon. The temple, made entirely of Pentelic marble, was amphiprostyle and tetrastyle, which means that it has four Ionic columns (4.66 metres high) on the front and another four on the back. The three-stepped crepis on which it stood enhances its distinctive Attic elegance and grace.

Part of the parapet from the temple of Athena Nike

Represented on the east side of its frieze were the gods of Olympus with Athena at the centre, between Zeus and Poseidon. The subjects on the other sides were battles between Greeks or between Greeks and Persians. The reliefs of the north and west sides are in the British Museum and those on the temple are replicas. The monument was demolished by the Turks in order to build a bastion, but fortunately its building material was found in 1834 and so its reconstruction was possible.

View of the temple of Athena Nike, from the east

Mourning Athena

In the late fifth century BC the tower was revetted on three sides by a parapet one metre high. Its exterior was adorned with reliefs of exquisite art (some are in the Acropolis Museum), representing animated winged Nikai in light and airy movements, preparing animals for sacrifice and trophies for victories, which were offered to Athena, who awaited at the centre, seated on a rock. One small Nike loosens her sandal, so as to step barefoot on the altar. The figures' garments cling to their lissom bodies and the vitality of their movements and pose of their wings give the impression that they are in flight.

Persons who passed through the Propylaia and entered the Acropolis beheld on the south side - to their right - the sanctuaries of Athena Hygeia and Artemis Brauronia (whose cult had been introduced by the deme of Brauron), as well as, just before the Parthenon, the Chalkotheke, in which bronze weapons and ships' rams were kept, all products of the craft of which Athena Ergane was patron deity. They would also have seen countless statues and ex-votos, on either side of the way along which the procession of the Panathenaia passed. On the left side, immediately opposite the Propylaia, towered the colossal bronze state of Athena Promachos, by the sculptor Pheidias, which together with its base stood 9 metres high. The tip of the goddess's spear glinting in the sun was reputed to be visible from out at sea.

THE PARTHENON

All the experience, wisdom and human effort of generations are crystallized in the Parthenon, the culminating architectural achievement of the ancient Greek spirit.

It is not known what rites were celebrated inside the temple of Athena, nor what role it played in the Panathenaia festival, since the peplos for Athena was destined for the cult effigy of her that stood in the Erechtheion. So the Parthenon should be regarded more as a political and cultural symbol than a religious one, given that its creator, Pericles, desired that the hegemony of Athens should be based primarily on her intellectual superiority.

The Parthenon was built on the summit of the Sacred Rock, on the spot where other temples of Athena had stood before it, including its immediate predecessor, which had been destroyed by the Persians in 480 BC, before it had been completed.

In 449 BC, Pericles commissioned the architect Iktinos and his collaborator Kallikrates to construct the Parthenon. It seems that Pheidias was "overseer" of all works, as well as the artistic creator of the temple's sculpted decoration. Building finished in 438 BC, while work on the sculptures continued until 432 BC. Originally the term Parthenon, which means chamber of Athena Parthenos, was used of the square room behind the cella, in which the public treasury was kept, and was later applied to the whole building.

The Parthenon is a Doric peripteral temple, with 8 x 17 columns 10.45   metres high. It is 69.71 metres long by 30.86 metres wide. The entire temple was

Horsemen from the north frieze of the Parthenon

The Moschophoros

dominated by architectural "refinements", which make it one of the most important buildings in the global architectural heritage: the columns swell at a short distance from their base and then taper towards the capital. This swelling is called entasis and imparts elasticity and vitality to the building.

Pitcher-bearers (hydriaphoroi) from the north frieze of the Parthenon

The axis of the columns is not perpendicular to the stylobate. All tilt towards the centre and the four corner columns have a double tilt, endowing the temple with the sense of a pyramid. This same movement is observed in the walls of the cella. Another of the refinements is the placement of the columns, which are not equidistant from each other. The line of the stylobate, and of its steps on the long sides, is also slightly curved, presenting a convexity of about 11 centimetres in the middle of the long sides and 7 centimetres in the middle of the narrow ones. These are ways of coping with the optical illusion, by which very long horizontal lines appear to sink in the middle, and also solve the problem of the shedding of rainwater. All these refinements were made to give the building life and movement, and they enhance not only the level of art in this period but also the aesthetic demands of the Athenian people.

Several parts of the original 92 metopes, the two pediments and the frieze around the cella survive. Most of them are now in the British Museum and a few in the Acropolis Museum. All are works by the great sculptor Pheidias and his pupils. The metopes on the east side represented the Gigantomachy (battle between gods and giants), on the south side the Centauromachy (battle between Lapiths and Centaurs), on the west the Amazonomachy (battle between Amazons and Athenians) and on the north the Trojan War - battles which reflected the mythical past and the recent conflict between the Greeks and the Persians.

The subject of the east pediment was the birth of Athena, who leapt fully-armed from the head of Zeus, to the astonishment of the assembled Olympian

Parthenon, part of the south colonnade

gods. The subject of the west pediment was the contest between Athena and Poseidon over the naming of the city. Poseidon offered the Athenians the spring of brackish water shown between his legs, and Athena the olive tree which dominated the centre of the scene. Athena won and gave her name to the city.

Unique masterpiece of sculpture was the Ionic frieze, 160 metres long, which surrounded the exterior of the cella. Some 600 figures of gods, mortals and animals were represented, participating in the procession of the Panathenaia. The procession commenced on the west side, with the preparation of the horsemen, and continued in parallel on the north and south sides, with men and women bearing offerings, and a host of animals for sacrifice, ascending to the Acropolis. The procession terminated on the east side, in the middle of which the gods and goddesses of Olympus, who had come to honour the great festival, awaited its arrival.

The cella of the Parthenon was named hekatompedos, because it was 100 Attic feet in length (approx. 30 m.), and was framed by three two-storey colonnades in Pi (Π) arrangement.

At the far end of the cella stood another magnificent creation of Pheidias, the colossal chryselephantine statue of Athena Parthenos, 10 metres high (12 m. including the base). The statue consisted of a wooden core, to which pieces of ivory were affixed for the flesh and hammered gold sheets for the garments and weapons. Athena was represented as a martial goddess, standing, her helmet intricately decorated with sphinxes and winged horses. On her chest she wore the aegis and in her right hand she held a winged Nike, 2 metres high. Her left hand rested on her shield, on the inner face of which was a coiled snake – the oikouros ophis of the Acropolis - as well as a scene of Gigantomachy. The outside of the shield was adorned with a scene of Amazonomachy. Represented on the soles of the goddess's sandals was the Centauromachy and on the base of the statue the birth of Pandora, with gold figures attached to the marble. It seems that the statue of Athena Parthenos was among those sculptures taken later to Constantinople, where it was destroyed by a fire in Late Antiquity.

The Parthenon suffered several interventions, when it was converted into a church, first of the Holy Wisdom (Hagia Sophia) and later dedicated to the Virgin of Athens (Panagia Atheniotissa) in Byzantine times. Under the Franks it became a Catholic church, from 1204, and under the Ottomans a mosque, from 1466. The Turks subsequently turned it into an ammunitions store, and on 26 September 1687, when the Venetian Doge Francesco Morosini bombarded the Acropolis from Philopappus Hill, a shell hit the Parthenon, causing a terrible explosion. Iktinos' masterpiece was reduced to a ruin. Shortly before the outbreak of the Greek War of Independence, in 1801-1803, Lord Elgin removed many of the monument's sculptures, which he later sold to the British Museum. Restoration works on the Parthenon began in 1975 and are still in progress.

Reconstruction of the northwest side of the Parthenon →

THE ERECHTHEION

The Erechtheion, on the north side of the Acropolis, impresses with its Attic elegance and grace. It stands on the most sacrosanct spot on the Rock, meeting point of the cults of many deities, such as Gaia, Hephaistos, Athena and Poseidon, and heroes, such as Kekrops, Erechtheus and Boutes.

The host of gods and heroes worshipped there, as well as the considerable difference in ground level, posed difficult problems for the unknown architect to solve. As a result, the Pentelic marble temple displays many architectural peculiarities, although as a whole it gives the impression of a harmonious unit.

The Erechtheion was built during the Peloponnesian War. Construction began in 421 BC and the monument was completed by the architect Philokles in 406 BC.

Erechtheion, detail

The east porch with the six slender Ionic columns led into the temple of Athena, in the cella of which was the olive-wood cult effigy (xoanon) of the goddess, which was believed to have fallen from heaven. It was this xoanon that was robed with the peplos embroidered by Athenian maidens, during the celebration of the Panathenaia. In front of the statue was the undying flame, in a gold lamp created by the artist Kallimachos.

On the north side of the temple there was a superb Ionic propylon with six lavishly decorated columns, which gave entry into the west part of the cella, which was dedicated to Poseidon and the hero Boutes.

The coffered ceiling of the propylon is a masterpiece of Attic art, as is the imposing portal framed by palmettes and rosettes,

The porch of the Korai or Karyatids on the Erechtheion

which were painted and embellished with gilded metal ornaments.

An aperture in the ceiling remained open, because it was believed to have been made by the thunderbolt of Zeus, which he hurled at Erechtheus, or by the trident of Poseidon, when he quarrelled with Athena and struck the ground, from which a spring of brackish water gushed forth. Correspondingly, there are three holes in the floor, which the ancient Greeks believed were trident marks.

A small entrance on the west side led to the temenos of the Nymph Pandrosos, where the olive tree that was Athena's great gift to the city grows. Next to the olive tree is the very ancient tomb of one of the mythical kings of Athens, Kekrops. It was possibly this tomb that was guarded by the six very beautiful Korai on the south side of the Erechtheion - those later named Karyatids, perhaps because they resemble the lovely maidens of the city of Karyai in Laconia, who performed ritual dances in honour of Artemis.

On their head they bear a kalathos, embellished with Ionic cymatium, upon which the roof of the porch rests. The slight flexing of one leg endows them with ease and grace, as if they are oblivious to the weight they support.

The four authentic Karyatids are exhibited in the Acropolis Museum, a fragmentary one is in the museum storerooms, while the sixth is in the British Museum.

Erechtheion, Karyatid

Reconstruction of the Erechtheion →

THE THEATRE OF DIONYSOS

The worship of Dionysos Eleutheros (from the city of Eleutherai, on the Attic-Boeotian border) was established officially in Athens in the sixth century BC, in the time of the tyrant Peisistratos. The Great Dionysia, a festival in honour of the god, which was held in the month of Elaphebolion and included theatrical performances, was soon instituted.

On the south slope of the Acropolis, within the sacred precinct of the god of wine and patron of theatrical art, the first theatre was created in the history of civilization, with wooden seats and a simple wooden skene. At the centre was a rectangular orchestra, where the ritual dance (chorus) took place around the altar of Dionysos, the thymele.

At first the rituals related to Dionysos' adventures, his death and resurrection, that is to vegetation and fertility in Nature, and their aim was to purify and to revive the life forces, with dances, with the impromptu rustic song, the dithyramb, and with mime performances. In fact, the word drama derives from all this action (Gr. drases). The male dancers in the chorus were dressed in goatskins and the song (Gr. ode) of the goats (Gr. tragoi) was the seed from which Tragedy sprouted.

In the sixth century BC, a great poet and actor appeared, Thespis from the Attic deme of Ikaria (pres. Dionysos), who introduced the first actor (hypokrites). His texts, which were recited by the actor and the chorus - whereas previously it had improvised - referred not only to the travails of Dionysos but also to the vicissitudes of other mythical and historical figures. Tragedy reached its peak in the fifth century BC, when Athens sired three great tragic poets, Aeschylus,

Reliefs from the so-called Bema of Phaidros

Zeus from the bema of Phaidros

Marble thrones from the theatre of Dionysos

Sophocles and Euripides, while concurrently Comedy was born, brilliant exponent of which was Aristophanes. All presented their immortal plays here, in the theatre of Dionysos.

The cavea was rebuilt of poros stone in the fourth century BC, in the archonship of Lykourgos, and acquired the form it has today, with 78 rows of seats and an estimated capacity of 17,000 persons. In the front row were 67 marble seats, reserved for the priests and pre-eminent citizens, while at the centre was the throne of the priest of Dionysos. In this phase of the theatre the orchestra became circular.

In Roman times the proscenium was extended into part of the orchestra, which became semicircular, while the skene was elaborated as a two-storey building. A little later, a parapet was built around the orchestra, as a protective barrier for spectators attending gladiatorial duels and contests with wild beasts. The orchestra was also often filled with water, for the staging of mock naval battles. In the early fifth century AD, a bema or dais for orators was set up in the orchestra. Known as the bema of Phaidros, it was decorated with a lovely relief from an earlier monument.

Votive relief

Reconstruction of the theatre of Dionysos →

THE ODEUM OF HERODES ATTICUS

Between the Theatre of Dionysos and the Odeum of Herodes Atticus extends the Stoa of Eumenes II, King of Pergamon, which was constructed by this great admirer of Athens in the second century BC. The stoa, which was 164 metres long and resembled the Stoa of Attalos in the Agora, served as a shelter for the theatre audience in the event of bad weather and as a place for a stroll.

Herodes Atticus, a noble and wealthy Athenian from the deme of Marathon, who lived in the second century AD, was a gifted   orator and teacher of many sophists and various personalities of the age, among them the future emperor Marcus Aurelius.

Among the many monuments and public works that Herodes Atticus built as benefactions all over Greece was the odeum, a roofed theatre for musical performances, which he erected in AD 161, in memory of his dead wife Aspasia Annia Regilla, whom he loved excessively.

The skene is 35.40 metres long, the orchestra 18.80 metres in diameter and paved with black and white tiles of marble from Karystos, and the cavea, with 32 rows of seats, holds an audience of about 5,000. The roof was of cedar wood. The façade was three-storeyed with arched windows. The cavea has been rebuilt in Pentelic marble and each summer during the Athens Festival it fills with spectators attending performances of ancient drama, concerts, ballet and opera.

Reconstruction of the odeum of Herodes Atticus→

THE ANCIENT AGORA

Dominating the west side of the Agora is the all-marble temple of Hephaistos, which stands on the hill of Agoraios Kolonos. The monument, like the surrounding area, is commonly known as the Theseion, since it was formerly thought to have been dedicated to Theseus, but is now known to have been dedicated to Hephaistos and Athena, whose cult statues, works by the great sculptor Alkamenes, stood in its cella. Traces of workshops and furnaces have been found on the slopes of the hill and Hephaistos was patron deity of smiths. Athena too was patroness of craftsmen and especially potters (Gr. kerameoi), after which the adjacent quarter of Kerameikos is named.

The Hephasteion was built shortly after the mid-fifth century BC, by the same unknown architect as designed the temples of Poseidon at Sounion, of Nemesis at Rhamnous and of Ares in the Agora. It is in the Doric order and peripteral, with 6 x 13 columns. The cella is amphiprostyle in antis, and it has a pronaos and an opisthodomos. The construction displays some of the refinements of the Parthenon: the columns have slight entasis and incline slightly towards the centre. Predominant theme of the temple's sculptural decoration are the Labours of Herakles and of Theseus, which are represented on the metopes. The subject of the internal frieze is the Centauromachy, as well as Theseus' battle against his cousins the Pallantids, sons of Pallas, who claimed the throne of Athens. Some pieces of the pedimental sculptures, which probably represented Centauromachy and the Apotheosis of

Theseion, temple of Hephaistos

Reconstruction of the Tholos, seat of the prytaneis, in the Agora of Athens →

The grave stele of Dexileos in the Kerameikos

Herakles, are exhibited in the Stoa of Attalos. After the prevailing of Christianity, the temple was converted into a church of St George, which continued in use until 1834, when the edifice was declared a national monument.

The word agora derives from the verb ageiro, which means to assemble, to congregate. Thus, the Agora was not just a marketplace for trading transactions but also a meeting place for citizens, the heart of the civic life of Athens, with public services and governmental buildings. And although the paramount religious centre of the city was the Acropolis, there were sanctuaries in the Agora too, as well as statues of mythical and historical figures.

The Tholos, the circular base of which can be seen at the foot of Agoraios Kolonos Hill, was the seat of administration of the city-state. The 50 prytaneis, who were one-tenth of the bouleutai, took their meals in the Tholos and some resided there, on the alert. It was built around 470 BC to replace an earlier edifice that had been destroyed by the Persians.

North of the Tholos was the New Bouleuterion, a building of the fifth century BC, the meeting place of the Boule of 500, which drafted laws that were voted on by the Ekklesia of the Deme. East of it are the foundations of the Metroon, the sanctuary of the Mother of the Gods, which also housed the state archive.

In front of these buildings is a high marble pedestal on which stood bronze statues of the Ten Eponymous Heroes, after whom the ten tribes of Attica are named. On the front of the pedestal wooden plaques were hung, on which public announcements were written, such as proposed legislation, conscription lists, and so on.

Beyond the Metroon was the small fourth-century BC temple of Apollo with the epithet Patroos, because he was father (Gr. patros) of Ion, genarch of the Ionians.

Reconstruction of the temple of Zeus Olympios →

Adjacent to it is a Π-shaped stoa, in which Zeus was worshipped as god of freedom (Eleuthereus). Beside the modern electric-train tracks stood the Royal (Basileios) Stoa, seat of the Archon Basileus, while on the north side, by Adrianou Street, was the Painted (Poikile) Stoa, which was decorated with wall-paintings, known as the philosophers' meeting place (enteukterion). It was frequented by Zenon from Kition in Cyprus, founder of the School of Stoics, who took their name from this stoa.

In font of the Stoa of Zeus Eleuthereus stood the fifth-century BC temple of Ares, to the north of it the Altar of the Twelve Gods, and to the south of it the odeum built by Marcus Vispanius Agrippa in the first century BC. In the early fifth century AD this odeum was incorporated in an enormous building which was formerly thought to be a Gymnasium or venue of philosophical schools, but which was probably a commandery or a residence linked with the Athenian Empress Eudokia, wife of Theodosios II the Younger. The colossal statues of one Giant and two Tritons, which adorned its propylon, were spolia taken from the odeum.

On the south side of the Agora were three stoas, the Middle, the East and the North, to the west of which was perhaps the most formal Attic law-court, the Heliaia, or, according to a more recent view, the sacred Aiakeion.

The east side of the Agora is defined by the Stoa of Attalos, which was erected by the homonymous King of Pergamon, in the second century BC. This two-storey monument, 116.50 metres long and 19.50 metres deep, has been restored completely and now houses many of the interesting finds from the Agora.

In Roman times Athens was adorned with a further two monuments: the Library of Hadrian, an enormous building complex with a theatre, lecture halls and garden with cistern, and the Roman Agora or forum, prominent feature of which is the Horologion built by the astronomer Andronikos Kyrrhestes, which was both a water clock and a wind-vane. On each side of this octagonal tower are relief personifications of the winds, which is why the monument is popularly known as the Tower of the Winds or Aerides.

The clock-tower (horologion)
of Andronikos Kyrrhestes

Reconstruction of the Library of Hadrian →

S ounion is 67 kilometres southeast of Athens, at the very end of the Attic Peninsula. The cape is crowned by the white columns of the ancient temple, in perfect harmony with the beautiful landscape. From here there is a vista of the Attic coast, the islets, the Cyclades and the mountains of the Peloponnese. The sunset is spectacular.

The headland was evidently inhabited from early times. Graves and other finds point to the presence of a prehistoric settlement in the third millennium BC. Sounion apparently became a religious centre very early too, since Homer describes the cape as sacred. Many gods and heroes were worshipped here, but the main ones were Athena and Poseidon.

The Athenians were quick to realize the strategic importance of the promontory and fortified it, in order to control the sea routes to the islands and primarily to Euboea, along which passed the cargoes of grain, staple foodstuff of the population of Athens. Primarily, however, the Athenians wanted to protect the major source of their wealth, the precious mines of argentiferous lead in nearby Laurion. It was with the income from the Laurion mines that the Athenians could afford to build, at the behest of Themistokles, 200 trieremes, with which they defeated and destroyed the Persian fleet in the naval battle of Salamis in 480 BC. So the Athenians constructed on the summit of the cape a semicircular wall, 500 metres long and over 3 metres wide, reinforced by square towers at 20-metre intervals. In the sea, on the northwest side, they dug the rock and constructed a small ship-shed (neorion) for two trieremes, which patrolled the waters.

The sanctuary of Poseidon was entered through a monument-al propylaia on its northeast side. To the right lie the ruins of a square hall, which was perhaps the guardhouse, beyond which are the ruins of two stoas, one at right angle to the other, in which pilgrims congregated during festivals, especially if there was bad weather.

The temple of Poseidon was built after the mid-fifth century BC, to replace the earlier poros temple, which fell victim to the Persian invaders in 480 BC. The white marble for the temple was quarried locally, at Agrileza near Sounion, on Laureotic Olympos, and lacks those constituents of Pentelic marble, which endowed the Acropolis monuments with the distinctive warm golden hue. It is also less durable and is eroded continuously by salt spray from the sea. For this reason the architect made the columns with shallower flutes and reduced their number from the usual 20 to 16.

Although the identity of the architect is unknown, he is surely the same one as

View of the temple of Poseidon, from above

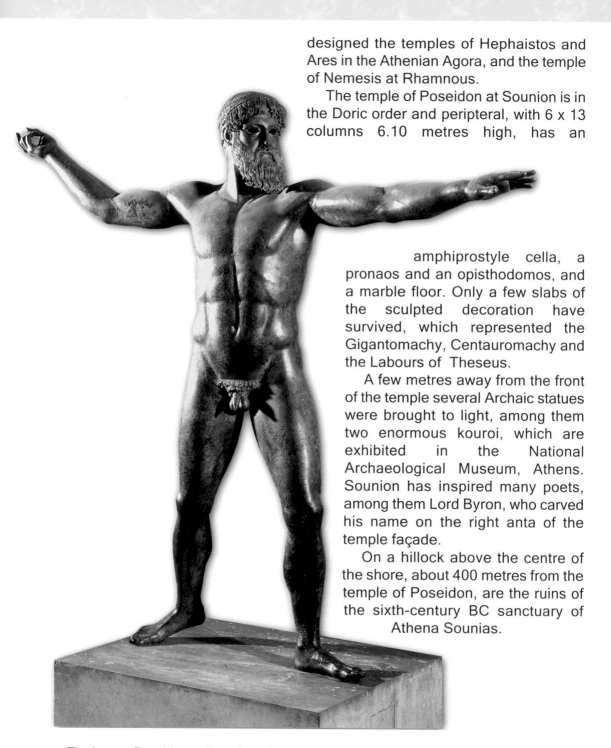

designed the temples of Hephaistos and Ares in the Athenian Agora, and the temple of Nemesis at Rhamnous.

The temple of Poseidon at Sounion is in the Doric order and peripteral, with 6 x 13 columns 6.10 metres high, has an amphiprostyle cella, a pronaos and an opisthodomos, and a marble floor. Only a few slabs of the sculpted decoration have survived, which represented the Gigantomachy, Centauromachy and the Labours of Theseus.

A few metres away from the front of the temple several Archaic statues were brought to light, among them two enormous kouroi, which are exhibited in the National Archaeological Museum, Athens. Sounion has inspired many poets, among them Lord Byron, who carved his name on the right anta of the temple façade.

On a hillock above the centre of the shore, about 400 metres from the temple of Poseidon, are the ruins of the sixth-century BC sanctuary of Athena Sounias.

The bronze Poseidon or Zeus from Artemision

Reconstruction of the temple of Poseidon →

AEGÎNA

T he beginnings of the history of Aegina are lost in the mists of time. Certainly the island was inhabited in the Neolithic Age, by settlers from the Peloponnese.

Originally named Oinone, myth has it that it was called Aegina when Zeus - or Aias according to another version - abducted the daughter of the river-god Asopos, Aegina, and brought her to the island, where she gave birth to the sage Aiakos. Aiakos was famed for his justice and became one of the three judges in Hades, together with Minos and Rhadamanthys.

In historical times, the Aeginetans were highly successful merchants and mariners. They ploughed the sea lanes from the Western Mediterranean to the Euxine Pontus and in the sixth century BC struck the first silver coins, the "turtles", which together with the weights and measures of Aegina were diffused throughout the Mediterranean and kept their value until Roman times. Aegina was destroyed because of its rivalry with Athens and from 390 BC onwards is only mentioned sporadic-ally in history.

Of the many monuments of various periods existing on the island, the most renowned is the temple of Aphaia, which stands on an eminence some 300 metres high, overlooking the bay of Aghia Marina.

The cult of Aphaia seems to have come from Crete (where she was also known as Britomartis - the Cretan Artemis - or Diktynna), in the course of the trading relations between the two islands.

According to tradition, Aphaia was a noble maiden from Crete, who, to escape the amorous advances of Minos, boarded an Aeginetan ship. But because the sailors also began to harass her, she leapt into the sea and came ashore on Aegina, where she disappeared from their sight into the woods, became invisible (a-phaia).

The temple, built in the early fifth century BC, is in the Doric order, 15.50 metres wide by 30.50 metres long, peripteral with 6 x 12 columns, with pronaos and opisthodomos in antis, which communicated with the cella in which the cult statue of the goddess was protected by a wooden railing all around.

The temple was built of local poros stone, except for the pediments and the roof, which were of marble. Some of the poros columns, 5.272 metres high, are monolithic and others have drums.

The statues on both pediments represent scenes from the two Trojan campaigns, in which the Aiakids distinguished themselves. Athena was the central figure on both pediments; represented symmetrically to right and left of

The corner colonnade of the temple of Aphaia

her are battles between Herakles and the Trojans, on the east pediment, and between Agamemnon and Trojans, on the west.

Seventeen of these statues have been revealed and are now in the Glyptothek in Munich.

Detail of the Doric column in the temple of Aphaia

Reconstruction of the temple of Aphaia on Aegina →

CORINTH

ncient Corinth was an important crossroad between continental Greece and the Peloponnese, and between the Aegean and the Ionian Sea. Its privileged location, fertile plain and abundant water sources attracted human habitation already from the Neo-lithic Age.

The rich prehistory of the region is reflected in the equally rich mythological tradition. According to one myth, the city was founded by the wily Sisyphos, symbol of the Corinthians' entrepreneurial spirit. Reputed to have deceived gods and men in his lifetime, in the end he succeeded in deceiving death itself. But Hermes Psychopompos arrested him and led him to Hades, where he was condemned to push for all eternity an enormous boulder towards a mountaintop. On the summit of the Acrocorinth, Bellerophon tamed Pegasos, and with the help of this mythical winged horse annihilated the terrible monster, the Chimaera.

Corinth was also the setting for the tragedy of Medea, who murdered her two children in order to avenge her fickle husband, when he abandoned her to marry the princess Glauke. The vengeful Medea sent Glauke a poisoned robe, which when she donned it enveloped her in flames. In order to save herself, the unfortunate Glauke fled to the waters of the spring that has borne her name ever since.

In the second millennium BC Corinth was inhabited by Hellenic tribes, while in the eleventh century BC Dorians settled here and their leader Aletes is mentioned as the first king. One of his descendants, Bakchis, founded the Bakchiad dynasty, which ruled the city from the ninth to the seventh century BC, bringing it to great prosperity. It was then that the Diolkos was constructed at the Isthmus, a paved road over which ships were hauled from the Saronic to the Corinthian Gulf and vice versa, and the great mercantile fleet of Corinth was created. Bronzes and the famous Corinthan vases were exported from the city to the whole of the Mediterranean, while concurrently wealthy colonies such as Corcyra and Syracuse were founded. Corinth was the largest commercial centre in western Greece.

During the seventh century BC, the Bakchiads were succeeded by Kypselos and his son Periander, who was one of the Seven Sages of Antiquity and is also accredited with the maxim **"Democracy is better than Tyranny"**. He banned the slave market, supported the poor and patronized the Arts and Letters. Under his guidance Corinth developed into a major cultural and intellectual centre. Kypselos was also the first to conceive the idea of cutting through the Isthmus. But his plans (like those of Demetrios Poliorketes, Julius Caesar and Nero) in this direction were not implemented and the Diolkos seems to have

The Corinth Canal

The Roman odeum of ancient Corinth

remained in use for several centuries more.

In Hellenistic times Corinth was one of the most populous cities in Greece, a busy centre of culture and commerce. There was a saying that "not everyone can travel to Corinth", on account of the high cost of staying there.

In 146 BC, the Roman forces commanded by Lucius Mummius defeated the army of the Achaian Confederacy, under General Diaios, and razed Corinth to the ground. This victory was decisive for the subjugation of Greece to Rome.

For almost one hundred years the city was literally erased from the map, until 44 BC when Julius Caesar, realizing its strategic importance, rebuilt it and renamed it Laus Julia Corinth-iensis, establishing it as administrative centre of the Roman province of Greece. The new city rapidly grew into a cosmopolitan centre populated by Greeks, Romans, Jews and Phoenicians, each worshipping their own gods. Apostle Paul organized at Corinth one of the first Christian communities in Europe, to which he addressed his renowned Epistles to the Corinthians.

From the third century AD the city suffered a series of destructions due to earthquakes and barbarian attacks, and its inhabitants gradually left to seek refuge on the Acrocorinth.

Outside the archaeological site of Corinth, to the west is the odeum, which was built in the first century AD and was partially revetted with marble by Herodes Atticus in the second century AD. Further north is the theatre, which was remodelled in various phases, between the fifth century BC and Roman times. In the site, on the left before the museum, are two monuments, the Glauke Spring, dug in the rock, and the temple of Apollo, of the sixth century BC, with 6 x 15 Doric monolithic columns, seven of which still stand.

To the southeast spreads the agora, which was the focus of trading transactions and public affairs. An immense rectangular area (225 x 127 m.), paved with flagstones, it acquired its final form in the first century BC, under Julius Caesar. On the west edge of the agora is a row of 12 shops, in front of

Reconstruction of the Archaic temple of Apollo →

which stand six small temples, dedicated to Poseidon, Herakles, Tyche and other deities, as well as the pedestal that bore the monument of the archon Babbius Philinus. On the south side are a further 29 shops, the line of which is interrupted by the bema from which orators delivered speeches.

Behind the shops is the South Stoa, of the fourth century BC, in which there was accommodation for representatives of the Greek cities attending the assemblies (synedria) convened by Philip II of Macedon and his son Alexander the Great. Behind the South Stoa are various administrative buildings, such as the South Basilica, next to which commenced the road to the harbour of Kenchreai on the Saronic Gulf.

The east side of the agora was delimited by the city archive and the Julian Basilica, in which were found statues of members of the Julian family, to which Julius Caesar and Augustus belonged. The north side was defined by a row of 15 shops, of which the arch of the central one has survived.

To the east are the propylaia, the monumental entrance to the agora at the end of the road from Lechaion, the second harbour of Corinth, on the Corinthian Gulf. The propylaia were adorned with statues of Helios and Phaethon, who were the   patron deities of the city. Just to the east of the propylaia was the Peirene Fountain, a building of the sixth century BC, which was renovated by Herodes Atticus in the second cen- tury AD.

Preserved behind the fountain-house and east of the road to Lechaion are columns from the precinct of Apollo, which was used for public religious gatherings, while further north are the baths of Eurykles, which Pausanias described as the loveliest in Corinth.

Ruins of the temple of Octavia at Corinth

Reconstruction of the Peirene Fountain→

EPIDAUROS

T he most renowned Asklepieion or sanctuary of Asklepios in the Hellenic world, to which people came in hope of a cure from serious illnesses, was located 10 kilometres away from the city of Epidauros.

According to myth, King Phlegyas came to Epidauros from Thessaly, in order to reconnoitre the region, with the intention of conquering it. His daughter Koronis lay with the god Apollo and conceived Asklepios. However, because she united also with a mortal, Ischys, Apollo ordered his sister Artemis to kill Koronis and throw her into the fire. Apollo snatched his son Asklepios from her vitals and handed him over to Hermes, who took the infant to Pelion, where the Centaur Cheiron undertook his upbringing and taught him the healing art.

According to another mythological tradition, Asklepios originated from Boibe on the Plain of Dotios, west of northern Pelion, and was the son of Koronis, daughter of King Phlegyas. He studied medicine in Cheiron's school and then settled at Trikke (Trikala), where he founded the first Asklepieion. His cult found fertile ground at Epidauros because there, on the summit of Mount Kynortion, Maleatas, a local deity with therapeutic qualities, had been worshipped already from Mycenaean times. The two gods were amalgamated into the deity known as Apollo Maleata. From the sixth century BC, the cult was established in the well-known sanctuary on the plain.

The patients who arrived at the sanctuary of Asklepios first washed in the sacred spring and then were put on a diet. They offered a sacrifice to the god and discussed their affliction with the priests. They participated in mystical rites that prepared them for their communication with the god and then spent the night in the special dormitory known as the Abaton or Enkoimeterion. It was believed that there the god visited the sick, usually in the form of a

Statues of the Roman period, in the Epidauros Museum

The ground floor space of the stoa of the Abaton, after reconstruction of the colonnade

snake, and healed them. The natural environment and the faith of the patients perhaps contributed to the success of certain cases. However, the enormous experience acquired by the priests soon led them to apply more serious therapeutic methods.

The ill gave money and votive offerings, and thus great wealth accumulated in the sanctuary over the years. This was used to construct splendid monuments, mainly during the fourth and third centuries BC. The Romans respected the sanctuary, with the exception of Consul Sulla, who shared its fabulous riches with his soldiers, in 86 BC.

In the fifth century AD, Emperor Theodosios II issued an edict closing the ancient sanctuaries, while the final blow of destruction was dealt to the Asklepieion of Epidauros by terrible earthquakes in the sixth century AD.

The theatre of Epidauros, which dominates the southeast sector of the archaeological site, was designed by the architect Polykleitos the Younger from Argos, in the fourth century BC. Pausanias mentions that this theatre surpassed all others in beauty and harmony. It was attuned perfectly to the landscape and this adaptation to the natural setting also accounts for its perfect acoustics. The cavea is divided into a lower and an upper diazoma, with 34 and 21 rows of seats respectively. The upper diazoma is considered to be an addition of Hellenistic times, which enlarged the capacity of the theatre from 6,200 to 12,300 spectators. The shape of the orchestra, unlike that of the cavea, is a perfect   circle, of 20.30 metres diameter. At its centre stood the altar.

The skene was a two-storey construction 26.15 metres long with proscenium,

Reconstruction of the ancient theatre of Epidauros →

Corinthian column capital, model for the internal colonnade of the Tholos

Detail of the decoration of the roof of the Tholos

the façade of which was adorned with 18 Ionic columns. Between the orchestra and the skene are passages, the parodoi, which are in the form of propyla. Since 1954, the theatre has been used for performances, featuring Maria Callas, Melina Mercouri and other great Greek and international artists.

The sanctuary was entered through the propylaia on the north side, which were built in the fourth century BC. From there the sacred way led to the temple of Asklepios, which was constructed in the fourth century BC by the architect Theodotos.

It was in the Doric order, peripteral, with 6 x 11 columns, and comprised a pronaos and a cella. Inside the cella stood the chryselephantine cult statue of the god, work of the sculptor Thrasymedes. The decoration of the exterior and the sculptures on the pediments are attributed to the sculptor Timotheos.

Visible to the west of the temple are the circular foundations of the Tholos or Thymele, which was the most magnificent edifice in the sanctuary. It was erected in the fourth century BC by Polykleitos the Younger, who used diverse materials in its construction – poros stone, black and white marble. It comprised a circular cella, encircled by two colonnades, an external of 26 Doric columns and an internal of 14 Corinthian. The ceiling was of marble, with carved flowers in the coffers, while the floor was paved with black and white lozenge-shaped marble tiles. The interior walls of the cella were

Reconstruction of the north propylon of the sanctuary of Asklepios→

decorated with murals painted by Pausias in the encaustic technique. Beneath the floor there was a labyrinth, which was perhaps associated with the worship of chthonic deities.

The entire north side of both the Tholos and the temple was closed by a long narrow building, the Abaton or Enkoimeterion, in which the sick spent the night, awaiting the god's visitation.

To the southeast of the temple are the foundations of a small Doric prostyle temple dedicated to Artemis, dating from the fourth century BC. This is followed by the ruins of the ceremonial banqueting hall, the hestiatorion, also known as the gymnasium, which dates from the late fourth or the early third century BC, inside which a small odeum was built in Roman times. Further south are the remains of the Greek bathhouse, of the third century BC, and to the east of it the Xenonas or Kataphygion, a large "hotel" with over 150 rooms, of the third century BC.

Last, as visitors walk along the road towards the theatre they encounter the stadium of the fourth century BC, the track of which is 181.10 metres long and unlike other stadia has no semicircular sphendone.

The Stadium

Reconstruction of the Tholos of Epidauros$\rightarrow$

MYCENAE

Tradition has it that Mycenae was founded by Perseus, son of Danae and Zeus, who had metamorphosed into golden rain in order to impregnate her. Perseus, after accidentally killing his grandfather, King Akrisios of Argos, fled and searched for a suitable place in which to found a new city. When he reached this site, he picked a mushroom (Gr. mykes), and from under it gushed a spring of water. According to an- other version of the myth, the pommel (Gr. mykes) fell off his sword, which was taken as a divine sign to build "Mykenes" (Mycenae) here.

Then, with the help of the Cyclops, the giants with one eye at the centre of the forehead, he girt the citadel with the "Cyclopean walls", as the circumvallation was dubbed later by the Greeks of the historical period, because they did not believe that ordinary men could have moved the enormous boulders used to build it. Perseus and his wife Andromeda had many children and created the dynasty of the Perseids.

However, the great heyday of Mycenae coincides with the dynasty of the Atreids, which succeeded the Perseids. The brothers Atreus and Thyestes came to Mycenae from Pisa in the western Peloponnese, whence their father had banished them for murdering their brother Chrysippos.

But their unquenchable thirst for power led them to heinous crimes and civil strife. Atreus' wife Aerope committed adultery with Thyestes. Atreus killed Thyestes' children and served them up to him at a feast. Atreus' sons, Agamemnon and Menelaus, went to Sparta, where they married the daughters of King Tyndareus, Clytaemnestra and Helen, respectively.

Agamemnon returned to Mycenae and became king. In the meanwhile the Trojan War broke out, which is described in *Homer's Iliad*. Among the booty brought home by Agamemnon was the princess of Troy Cassandra, who

Gold cup from Mycenae

The Lion Gate of Mycenae

Representative examples of grave goods from Grave Circle A

had already borne him two children. Thyestes' son, Aegisthus, who had been Clytaemnestra's paramour during her husband's absence, murdered Agamemnon, Cassandra and their two children. Eight years later, Orestes, son of Agamemnon and Clytaemnestra, returned to Mycenae to avenge his father's death, killing his mother and Aegisthus. He then married Hermione, daughter of Menelaus, and fathered Tissamenos, the last scion of the Atreids.

In 1876, Heinrich Schliemann brought to light Grave Circle A', proving the existence of the Mycenaean Civilization and the historicity of the Homeric epics, which no one believed in until then. A major step in the study of this civilization was made in 1952, with the decipherment by Michael Ventris and John Chadwick of Linear B script, which is inscribed on clay tablets found in many Mycenaean palaces.

The lower city, around the citadel, is full of ruined houses and clusters of tombs. As visitors walk up to the citadel, they see on the left, cut into the bedrock, the so-called chamber tombs, in which the families of city-dwellers were buried.

They come next to the Tomb of Agamemnon or Treasury of Atreus, as Pausanias called it in the second century AD, because people at that time believed it contained the treasures of Atreus and his sons.

According to the latest dating, it was constructed around 1250 BC. It is the largest of the so-called tholos or beehive royal tombs that occur in abundance all over Greece. Nine of these are at Mycenae and most were found looted. The

Reconstruction of the Tholos Tomb of Atreus→

dromos of the tomb is 36 metres long and 6 metres wide, and its walls are built of isodomic masonry.

The lintel consists of two enormous stones, the inner one of which weighs 122 tons, above which is the "relieving triangle" built in the corbelling system. One slab covered the outer face of the relieving triangle, with a relief decoration.

The entrance was flanked by engaged columns of greenish stone, decorated with spirals and bands, parts of which are exhibited in the National Archaeological Museum, Athens.

The double wooden door was closed after the burial and the dromos filled in with earth. The circular chamber is of corbelled construction, with 33 courses of stones, each course projecting slightly above the underlying one and thus forming the tholos, which was closed at the apex by a large keystone. The tholos was 13.40 metres high and 14.60 metres in diameter at its base. Bronze rosettes were affixed to the walls.

The dead were placed on the ground, along with their favourite personal possessions. The treasury also has a rock-cut side chamber.

As visitors approach the citadel, they see on the right ruins of houses, known today by conventional names, such as the House of Shields, the Oil Merchant's House, etc., given to them by the

Gold mask from Grave Circle A' and other precious finds

Reconstruction of Grave Circle A' →

Stone vases from the House of Shields

excavators, on the basis of certain characteristic finds recovered from them. Outside the citadel, to the west and on the approaching visitors' right, is Grave Circle B, which includes 24 graves in which many precious objects, dating from the seventeenth and the early sixteenth century BC, were discovered. In proximity to Grave Circle B are another two tholos tombs, known conventionally as the tombs of Aegisthus and of Clytaemnestra. The first is dated circa 1500 BC and the second circa 1220 BC.

The citadel of Mycenae covers an area of 30,000 square metres and is enclosed by Cyclopean walls 900 metres long, of estimated height 12 metres and varying in thickness from 3 to 9 metres. For the most part they are built of huge boulders, with smaller stones filling the joins and no mortar. Building of the citadel began in the mid-fourteenth century BC and it acquired its final form after various modifications, in the late thirteenth century BC.

The Lion Gate was constructed around 1250 BC and consists of two vertical monolithic jambs and the lintel weighing about 12 tons. The relieving triangle is covered by a limestone slab carved in relief with two confronted lionesses,

Reconstruction of part of the palace of Mycenae →

Rock-crystal duck-shaped vase from Grave Circle B

The "Warrior krater" from Mycenae

The wall-painting known as "The Lady of Mycenae", from the Cult Centre

presumably symbolizing the power of Mycenae, and between them a column, symbolizing a deity or perhaps the palace.

The heads of the heraldic beasts were probably of steatite and no longer exist.

Inside the gate, on the right, are the ruins of the so-called granary, a three-storey building in the basements of which storage jars containing carbonized grain were found.

Immediately beyond is Grave Circle A, which was excavated by Heinrich Schliemann, who brought to light six royal shaft graves containing 17 skeletons of adult men and women, and two of children. The shaft graves were closed with wooden beams and covered with earth, on which was set a stone stele, sometimes bearing relief decoration. Abundant grave goods accompanied the burials.

Grave Circle A is a little later than Grave Circle B, the burials spanning the period 1600 to the early fifteenth century BC. In the thirteenth century BC, a low double wall of dressed slabs, with entrance, was built around the graves.

After the grave circle come the House of the Warrior Vase, the Ramp House and the South House.

Next are the Cult Centre, a complex that includes the Building of the Frescoes, the Building of the Idols, Tsountas' House, altars, the Processional Way, priests' houses, etc.

At the top of the hill stood the palace. Visitors first enter the large court, on the west side of which were the apartments for official guests.

The megaron consisted of a hall with two columns in antis, the prodomos and the domos, or megaron proper, with monumental hearth surrounded by four columns. The walls were decorated with frescoes.

A short way to the east of the megaron are the ruins of a few other buildings, which seem to have been annexes of the palace and storerooms.

There is a postern gate, imitating the Lion Gate, on the north side of the wall, while a portal on the northeast leads to the underground cistern.

The Oil Merchant's Quarter outside the Citadel

TIRYNS

T radition has it that the citadel of Tiryns was built by Proetus, who came from Lycia and brought the Cyclops with him. His son Megapenthes ceded his kingdom to Perseus, founder of Mycenae, taking in return the kingdom of Argos. Thus, the tradition of Tiryns is inextricably linked with that of Mycenae and of Argos.

Excavations have shown that Tiryns was inhabited in the Early Helladic period (3rd millennium BC). The first Mycenaean citadel was founded in the early fourteenth century BC, reconstructed and extended in the mid-thirteenth century BC and acquired its final form around 1200 BC.

In the fifth century BC, as Herodotus mentions, the Tirynthians took part in the battle of Plataiai (479 BC) against the Persians. Not long after, the Argeians destroyed both Tiryns and Mycenae.

The citadel of Tiryns was built on a low rugged hill and occupies an area 300 metres long by 45-100 metres wide. Its Cyclop-ean wall, reaching a height of 10 metres and varying in thickness from 8 to 10 metres, is a remarkable fortification work, which Pausanias (2nd c. AD) had no hesitation in comparing to the pyramids of Egypt.

To south and east of the wall are tunnels (syringes), with corbelled roofing and rooms at the rear. These are megalithic monuments of exceptional technique, which were presumably storerooms in peacetime and refuges in wartime.

The main entrance to the upper citadel is on the east side and there is a postern entrance on the west.

The palace is at the topmost point of the citadel. In front of the megaron is a

Clay figurine from the sanctuary in the Lower Citadel

Cyclopean syrinx-passage on the citadel of Tiryns

The Citadel of Tiryns

square court with colonnades around three sides.

The palace consists of the hall, the prodomos and the domos or megaron proper. On the right side of the domos, the king's throne stood on a dais. Four columns upheld the roof, around the circular hearth.

In the Geometric period (8th c. BC), a Doric temple believed to have been dedicated to Hera was erected on the site of the megaron.

East of the palace stood a smaller and earlier megaron with similar layout, which is conventionally called the "queen's megaron", and alongside this is a third, even smaller megaron.

West of the large megaron is the bathroom, the floor of which was a large limestone slab.

Around the megara were numerous other spaces, which intercommunicated via corridors and courts, and were used mainly as storerooms and workshops.

Reconstruction of part of the palace of Tiryns →

OLYMPIA

Olympia is located in an idyllic landscape in the western Peloponnese, in the pine-wooded vale of the River Alpheios and its tributary the Kladeos. From earliest times Olympia was a locus sanctus, where numerous deities were worshipped, among which the most important was Zeus, father of gods and men. However, Olympia owed its fame primarily to its games, the founding of which was associated with many myths in Antiquity.

According to one, Herakles held the first games in honour of his divine father Zeus, marked out the Hiera Altis (Sacred Grove) by planting trees all around, and defined the length of the Olympic stadium at 600 feet (192.27 m.).

According to another myth, Pelops, king of neighbouring Pisa, organized the games to commemorate his victory in the chariot race against Oinomaos, for which his prize was Oinomaos' daughter, Hippodameia.

After the reign of Oxylos, the games were neglected, until the accession of Iphitos to the throne of Elis. He consulted the Delphic oracle as to what to do to save Greece from wars and pestilence, and the oracle replied that the Eleians should revive the games at Olympia. Then Iphitos, together with Lykourgos of Sparta and Kleosthenes of Pisa, organized the games and instituted the Sacred Truce, that is the cessation of all hostilities for their duration.

Later, in 776 BC, Koroibos from Elis was victor in the stadion race. Henceforth, the Eleians began to record every four years the Olympiads, which were named each time after the winner in the stadion race. From the third century BC, this system became the fixed and most reliable basis of dating for the ancient Greeks.

Head of Antinoos at Olympia

Panoramic view of the archaeological site of Olympia

Terracotta disc-shaped akroterion from the Heraion

The adjudicators in the games were called Hellanodikai. From the noble lineages of Eleians were also elected the Spondophoroi ("libation-bearers"), who with herald's staff in hand and olive wreath on the head, travelled to the ends of the Hellenic world, to announce the onset of the Sacred Truce.

Thus the games became a national festival, uniting the whole of Hellenism, since Greeks from everywhere flocked to Olympia to attend not only the athletics games but also the artistic events, such as orations and recitations of works by great poets.

The glory of the Olympic Games continued unabated throughout Classical and Hellenistic times. King Philip II of Macedon competed in the equestrian contests and was victor in 356 BC. During the period of Roman rule, the games became ecumenical in character, whereas until then only Greeks had been permitted to participate.

The last Olympic Games in Antiquity were held in AD 393. The following year, Emperor Theodosios the Great abolished them. The sanctuary of Olympia suffered in later years and in the fifth century AD Theodosios II ordered the destruction of the temple of Zeus. Earthquakes and floods gradually relegated

Reconstruction of the Heraion of Olympia→

The Palaestra

the sanctuary to oblivion.

The Sacred Altis was delimited by a precinct wall (peribolos) 200 x 175 metres. A few metres beyond the entrance to the archaeological site, visitors encounter on the right the gymnasium of the second century BC, which consisted of a rectangular court and lateral stoas in which athletes trained for the running and throwing events.

At the southeast edge, a propylon in the Corinthian order linked it with the palaestra, a square building of the third century BC, in which athletes practised wrestling, boxing and jumping. Around the court were various rooms associated with athletics, such as the elaiothesion, the konisterion and so on.

Next comes the Theekoleon, seat of the sanctuary's administration or residence of priests, and the Heroon, with an altar dedicated to some unknown hero. Further west, near the river, were the "swimming pool" and bathhouse of the fifth century BC. Further south is the basilica that was built in the fifth century

Transverse section of the Temple of Zeus

The exedra of the Hellanodikai in the Stadium.

AD upon the ruins of Pheidias' Workshop, where the great sculptor created the ivory-and-gold statue of Zeus.

Next to this is the Leonidaion, a large "hotel" designed by the architect Leonides from Naxos, in the fourth century BC.

The South Stoa was erected in the same century. To the north of it is the bouleuterion, consisting of two apsidal buildings with an open space between them. There stood the statue of Zeus Orkios, where the athletes swore the oath of "fair play". The southeast building was a shrine that was demolished by Nero, in order to build his villa.

Further north is the Stoa of Echo or Heptaechos, 98 metres long, in which the voice was said to resound   or echo seven times. It housed many ex-votos and statues, and was decorated with mural paintings, from which reason it was also called Poikile.

Even today the stadium is entered via the cryptoporticus. The stadium could hold up to 45,000 spectators, who sat on the sloping ground. On the south side is the exedra of the Hellanodikai and directly opposite is the altar of Demeter

Reconstruction of the entrance to the Stadium →

The bull of Regilla from the Nymphaion.

Chamyne, whose priestess was the only woman who had the privilege of attending the games. The track, which is 600 ancient feet (i.e. 192.27 m.) in length, is marked by two stone starting lines (apheseis). The hippodrome, for the equestrian races, was situated to the south of the stadium, but has been washed away by the river.

On returning to the stadium, visitors see on the right the pedestals of the 16 Zannes, bronze statues of Zeus that were made from the fines levied on athletes who had violated the rules of the games.

Behind the Zannes, on a high terrace, stood the treasuries, for the safekeeping of precious ex-votos of cities, such as Sikyon, Selinous, Gela and others. West of the Zannes is the small Doric temple of Rhea or Cybele, Mother of the Gods, the Metroon, of the fourth century BC.

After the treasuries are the ruins of a monumental fountain, the Nymphaeum, which was built by Herodes Atticus in the second century AD. In its niches stood statues of eminent Romans and members of the magnate's family, and in the middle, between the two water tanks, stood a bull, a votive offering to Zeus from Regilla, Herodes' wife.

Reconstruction of the Nymphaion→

The temple of Hera (Heraion) was constructed in the late seventh century BC and originally had 6 x 16 wooden columns, which were replaced gradually by stone ones. It was in the Doric order, with pronaos, cella and opisthodomos.

The pediments were adorned with two terracotta akroteria in the form of discs. In the area between the Heraion and the temple of Zeus was the Pelopion, a tumulus with pentagonal peribolos, which was considered to be the cenotaph of the hero Pelops.

The temple of Zeus was built in 470-456 BC with booty taken by the Eleians when they destroyed Pisa. It was designed by the Eleian architect Libon and constructed of local shelly limestone, while the sculpted decoration was of Parian and Pentelic marble.

It was in the Doric order and

Hermes by Praxiteles, in the Olympia Museum

Reconstruction of the Temple of Zeus→

peripteral, with 6 x 13 columns, 10.40 metres high. Its interior comprised a pronaos, cella and opisthodomos, which does not communicate with the cella.

Circa 430 BC, the colossal chryselephantine statue of Zeus, work of Pheidias and one of the Seven Wonders of the ancient world, was set up inside the temple. This statue was taken to Constantinople in the fourth century AD, after which its traces vanished. Outstanding in front of the temple is the triangular pedestal of the Nike statue by Paionios, which is exhibited in the Olympia Archaeological Museum.

Close to the exit to the site is the circular base of the Philippeion, which Philip II of Macedon began building after the battle of Chaironeia, in 338 BC, and which was completed after his death, by his son Alexander. The cella was surrounded by 18 Ionic columns, parts of which have been restored recently, and it housed five chryselephantine portrait statues of members of Alexander's family.

A few metres to the north is the prytaneion, which housed the altar of Hestia, with the "undying flame". This was the seat of the prytaneis, the archons of the sanctuary, in which the Eleians offered a banquet in honour of the Olympic victors and foreign dignitaries.

The Nike by Paionios

Reconstruction of the Philippeion →

D elphi was an extremely important crossroads, between North and South, East and West, which partly justifies its characterization as "navel" (omphalos) of the earth. Situated on the southern slopes of Mount Parnassos, in one of the most spectacular landscapes in Greece, is the sanctuary of Apollo. According to mythology, Apollo came to this place and slew the dragon, Python, son of Gaia and symbol of the old religion.

In the Mycenaean period (1600-1100 BC), there was an organized settlement at Delphi and the oracle-shrine of Gaia was flourishing. Around 800 BC, worship of Apollo was introduced, while from the eighth to the fourth century BC the oracle-shrine enjoyed great fame. Its oracles influenced the decisions of individuals and of states, and were sought not only by Greeks but also be foreigners, such as King Croesus of Lydia and King Midas of Phrygia.

The sanctuary developed into an important religious and cultural centre, and was adorned with a host of monuments and ex-votos. In 600 BC the Pythia were instituted at Delphi, in honour of Apollo, initially as music contests and later as athletics games, when the festival was reorganized in 582 BC.

In the third century BC, Galatian hordes attacked the sanctuary, but were repelled by the Aetolians, who in their turn were expelled by the Romans. In

The navel of the earth (omphalos) at Delphi

A panoramic view of Delphi

View of the Gymnasium

Byzantine times, Constantine the Great transferred many ex-votos from Delphi to Constantinople. The oracle closed forever in AD 394.

The oracles were delivered according to a specific procedure: First, the Pythia was purified in the Kastalia Spring and entered the adyton (inner sanctum) of the temple of Apollo. She drank water from the spring, chewed laurel leaves and, seated upon a tripod, inhaled the vapours issuing from a fissure in the earth. She soon fell into an ecstatic trance and uttered unintelligible words. Special priests, the "Prophetai" interpreted these and delivered the oracle in metrical form. The answers were often ambiguous.

Excavations at the site commenced in 1891, under the direction of the French School of Archaeology at Athens. The Delphi Museum, which opened its doors in 1903, has been modernized recently. Today Delphi plays a notable cultural and intellectual role, as seat of the European Cultural Centre.

Located on the hillside known as Marmaria, before the sanctuary of Apollo, is the sanctuary of Athena Pronaia. The temple of Athena, built in the late sixth century BC on the site of an earlier one, was in the Doric order and peripteral, with 6 x 12

Reconstruction of the sanctuary of Athena Pronaia→

The sacred spring Castalia in the Roman times

columns. To the west of it stood two treasuries, one of which was in the Ionic order and built by the Massaliots in 530 BC.

Another important edifice is the Tholos, work of the fourth-century BC architect Theodoros. At the west edge of the sacred precinct is another Doric temple of the fourth century BC, perhaps dedicated to Athena and built after the destruction of the earlier one. Outside the sanctuary of Athena are the gymnasium, the palaestra and a circular bathhouse for athletes.

The sacred Kastalia Spring burbles at the foot of the Phaidriades Rocks. The water, which ran through lion-head spouts into a tank, had purificatory powers.

Just outside the main entrance to the sanctuary of Apollo are the ruins of a stoa that housed shops. Inside the gateway are several pedestals, after which visitors encounter the ruins of the treasuries, small temple-shaped buildings erected by the Greek cities in order to house precious ex-votos and commemorating a historical event. On the left are the foundations of the Sikyonian Treasury and next to it the Siphnian Treasury (6th. c. BC), with two Karyatids on the façade instead of columns.

There follow the treasuries of the Thebans, the Boeotians, the Megarians, the Syracusans and the Knidians. The Athenian Treasury was built of Parian marble to commemorate the establishment of Democracy, the Athenians' victory over the Persians in the Battle of Marathon. Northeast of it are the ruins of the Bouleuterion,

View of the Sacred Way with the Stoa of the Athenians right
and the Athenian Treasury in the background

The Naxian sphinx

and higher up is the temple of Gaia.

Next comes the Corinthian Treasury, which was put up by the tyrant Kypselos in the seventh century BC and is the earliest at Delphi.

Preserved to the left is the Stoa of the Athenians, 30 metres long and with seven columns on the façade, which housed booty from the Athenians' naval victories over the Persians.

Further up, beside the Sacred Way, stood the pedestals of gold tripods dedicated by the tyrants of Syracuse and of Gela, to commemorate their victory at Himera (480 BC), and the ex-voto of Daochos (373-331 BC).

Opposite the entrance to the temple of Apollo stands the altar to the god, ex-voto of the Chians.

The temple was built in the seventh century BC, but was destroyed by fire in 548 BC.

It was rebuilt by the Alkmeonids, but was destroyed again, by earthquakes, in 373 BC, after which the temple we see today was built by the famous architects Spintharos, Xenodoros and Agathon.

It was in the Doric order

Reconstruction of the temple of Apollo→

The Charioteer of Delphi

and peripteral, with 6 x 15 columns. The sculptural decoration on the pediments represented Apollo's arrival at Delphi (east pediment) and Dionysos with his retinue (west pediment).

A stairway leads up to the theatre of Delphi, which was constructed in the fourth century BC and acquired its final form in the Roman period. The cavea, with 35 rows of seats, could accommodate an audience of 5,000. A steep pathway leads up to the stadium, the stone seats of which had a capacity of 7,000 spectators, while the length of the track was 178.35 metres. The stadium is dated to the fifth century BC and it was here that the panhellenic Pythian Games were held.

The tiers of the theatre

DODONE

In a picturesque valley in Epirus, at the foot of Mount Tomaros, lies the oracle of Zeus Dodonaios, which was, according to ancient tradition, the oldest in Greece. During prehistoric times the Great Goddess, a fertility deity who later came to be known by the name Dione and formed a divine couple with Zeus, was worshipped here.

The "prophets" of the oracle, who interpreted the divine will, were called Selloi. They are described in the ancient sources as "aniptopodai", because they never washed their bare feet, and "chamaicuentai", because they slept on the bare ground. It seems that these habits were vestiges of the earlier chthonic cult of the Earth goddess Gaia, when the priests drew their oracular powers from her and were thus in direct contact with her. There is reference also to three aged priestesses, the Peleies. The turtledoves that nested in the sacred oak tree of the oracle were called Peleiads.

Initially, the oracles were based on the rustling of the leaves of the oak tree and the flight and cooing of the doves. Later, other means of divination were added, such as the sound produced by the bronze cauldrons set up in a ring around the oak.

After the mid-fourth century BC, the cauldrons were replaced by an ex-voto of the Corcyraians: a cauldron affixed to a colonnette and a statue of a child set upon a second colonnette. The child held a whip with three chains, which struck the cauldron as the wind blew.

The sanctuary began operating in the second millennium BC and continued to be frequented until the end of the fourth cen-tury AD. Citizens as well as communities sought the oracle's advice.

Distinguished figures such as Alexander the Great, Pyrrhos, Philip V of Macedonia, Hadrian and Julian the Apostate showed interest in Dodone in many ways. The sanctuary was destroyed by the Aetolians in 219 BC and the Romans in 167 BC. It was abandoned after the fifth-sixth century AD, on account of the Slav raids.

The first excavations at Dodone were conducted in 1875, by the Epirot antiquarian and politician C. Kapranos. The recent excavations began after 1950, under the direction of S. Dakaris, and are being continued by his former students.

The most impressive monument at Dodone is without doubt the excellent theatre, with a capacity of about 17,000. Its retaining wall is reinforced by towers built in the isodomic system. It was constructed in the early third century BC, during the reign of King Pyrrhos.

Destroyed by the Aetolians, it was rebuilt by Philip V of Macedonia in the late third century BC. In its final phase, in the reign of Emperor Augustus, it was converted into an arena.

East of the theatre stood a hypostyle hall, covering an area of 1,260 square metres and fronted by a Doric colonnade. This was the bouleuterion of the Koinon of Epirots. It was identified thanks to the altar close to the south wall, which had been dedicated to Zeus Naios and Bouleus, and Dione, by Charops, an eminent man of the time, who in 198 BC contributed to Flamininus' struggle in Epirus against the Macedonians.

The so-called Hiera Oikia ("Sacred Dwelling") is located in the middle of several buildings in amphitheatrical arrangement on the south slope of the hill. This is a rectangular precinct surrounded by a wall (peribolos), of dimensions 20.80 x 19.20 metres, in which four building phases can be distinguished. The original nucleus was a small temple with pronaos and cella, of the first half of the fourth century BC. According to ancient literary tradition, in olden days there were no walls, only the bronze cauldrons encircling the sacred oak tree.

In the early third century BC, in the reign of Pyrrhos (297-272 BC), the precinct wall was replaced by a larger construction with Ionic colonnades on three sides and an entrance in front.

When the Aetolians attacked Dodone, in 219 BC, they respected the Hiera Oikia because destruction of the sacred oak tree would have evoked the wrath of the whole of Hellas. Last, in 218 BC, the Macedonians and the Epirots, using the booty from their victory at Thermon in Aetolia, rebuilt the Hiera Oikia in monument-al style: in place of the small temple a larger one was erected, tetrastyle and in the Ionic order. In all probability an altar was set up on the site of the sacred oak tree.

South of the bouleuterion is the prytaneion, in the hearth of which burnt the undying flame. It was here that the prytaneis and other distinguished persons dined. The prytaneion consists of an original core, of the early third century BC, and an extension to this, of the late third century BC, which includes three chambers each equipped with nine benches, ancillary spaces, in which the archons dined, as well as an Ionic colonnade on the east face.

East of the bouleuterion, in addition to the Hiera Oikia there is a series of buildings, which are identified as follows: temple of Aphrodite, temple of Themis, old (330-324 BC) and new (post-219 BC) temple of Dione, Christian basilica and temple of Herakles (early 3rd c. BC).

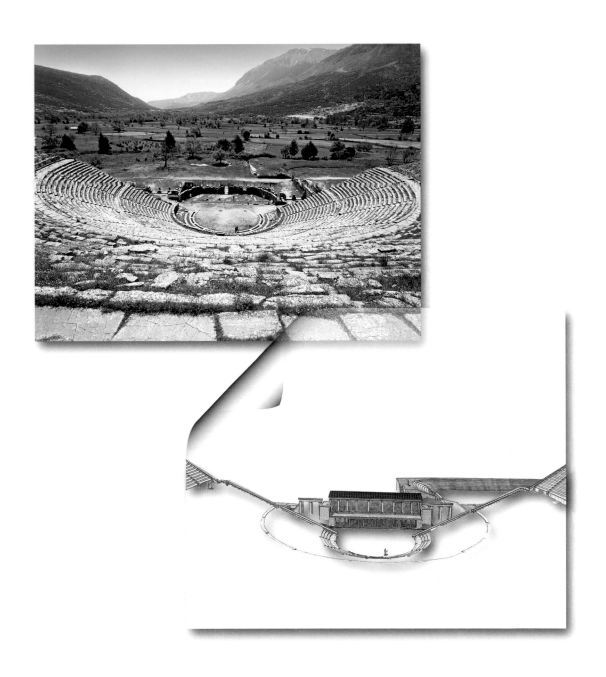

Reconstruction of the theatre of Dodone →

DION

The most official sanctuary of Zeus Olympios was founded at Dion by the Macedonians. The religious rites later came to include theatrical performances and athletics games, which acquired greater renown in the reign of Archelaos (413-399 BC).

In 348 BC, after Philip II had razed Olynthos to the ground, he came to Dion to glorify Zeus and to celebrate his victory. Alexander came here too, before embarking on his campaign into Asia, and held a great feast lasting nine days, as many as the number of the Muses. And when he defeated the Persians at the River Granikos, in 334 BC, he commissioned Lysippos to make 25 bronze statues of the Macedonians who fell in the battle, in order to dedicate them in the sanctuary of Zeus.

Over time, a city of some 15,000 inhabitants grew up close to the sanctuary. Its defensive walls - about 2,500 metres in length - were built in the late fourth century BC and rebuilt in the third century BC. The city suffered destructions at the hands of the Aetolians in the third century BC and the Goths in the fourth century AD, as well as from earthquakes, which brought its final abandonment.

Three female busts, as found near the altar in the sanctuary of Isis

Statue of Aphrodite Hypolympidia, which was found in situ

From the entrance to the archaeological site, a path leads to the sanctuary of the goddess Demeter. The earliest buildings are two temples of the fifth century BC, which were replaced by larger ones in the fourth century BC.

Proceeding eastwards, we come to the sanctuary of Isis, at the centre of which stands the temple of Isis, with four Ionic columns on the front. Isis was worshipped at Dion as "Lochia", protectress of childbirth, just as her predecessor Artemis Eileithyia. Two smaller temples either side of the central one, are of Isis Tyche and Aphrodite Hypolympidia respectively. Worship of Isis continued into Early Christian times.

Outside the walls of the city are the stadium, where athletics games took place, and the sanctuary of Zeus. A little further south is the small Roman theatre, built in the second century AD with stone seats and a skene with sculpted decoration. The large theatre of Dion acquired its present form in Hellenistic times. The seats in the cunei are built with large bricks, a unique example in Greece, and the orchestra is 26 metres in diameter.

Extra muros to the south lie the ruins of an Early Christian basilica of the fifth century AD. It was three-aisled with atrium, narthex and semicircular conch in the sanctuary. Just inside the entrance to the archaeological site are the ruins of the large thermae, which were built around 200 AD.

On the east side of this bath complex were a large assembly hall, changing rooms and a marble-lined swimming pool. On the north side stood statues representing the god of Medicine, Asklepios, and his family. Linked architecturally with the thermae was the odeum, which accommodated an audience of about 350.

A short distance to the north is the agora of Dion, which acquired its present form around AD 200. West of the agora are the ruins of the episcopal basilica, built upon the ruins of an earlier one of the fourth century AD, which was destroyed by earthquake.

Facing the main street is a monument of the fourth century BC, 37 metres in length and with reliefs of shields and breastplates, which was possibly the decoration of the façade of a building.

Dominating the east side of the city is the so-called Villa Dionysos, which is dated to the late second century BC. The bath installations occupy the south part, while at the centre is a large room also surrounded by baths and recreation chambers. Next comes a wing dedicated to the cult of Dionysos.

In the north part of the complex are two large peristyle courts, around which are the residential apartments, storerooms, etc. The most significant find is the superb mosaic floor of the symposium hall, with a scene of Dionysos standing in his chariot together with an aged Silenus.

The street through the agora is lined on one wide with shops and workshops. Excavations in the building complex opposite them, on the other side of the street, brought to light a unique find, a bronze musical instrument called a hydraulis ("water organ"), which is dated to the first century BC.

View of the Roman baths of Dion

A rchelaos, son of Temenos, King of Argos, pursued a she-goat (aix), as Apollo had counselled him, and the animal led him to the place where he founded Aigai. According to another version of the myth, Karanos, son of Pheidon, left Argos and came to Macedonia, where, obeying the instructions of a Delphic oracle, he followed a herd of goats. At the point where the herd stopped to sleep, Karanos founded Aigai. All these myths are fabricated to show that the Macedonian kings were descended from Herakles and his father Zeus, as well as from Temenos, King of Argos, which is why they were called Herakleids and Temenids.

When Archelaos I (413-399 BC) transferred the capital of the Macedonian State to Pella, for strategic reasons, Aigai lost none of its prestige. On the contrary, it enjoyed its heyday in the fourth century BC. Moreover, it remained the burial place of the Macedonian kings. Sole exception was Alexander the Great, who died in distant Babylon and was buried in Alexandria.

In 276 BC, Antigonos Gonatas ascended the throne of Macedonia and clashed with Pyrrhos, King of Epirus, who defeated him and conquered Aigai. In 168 BC, the city was sacked by the Romans and subsequently lost its glory. With the passage of time, both the name and the site of Aigai were forgotten.

In 1861 the French archaeologist Léon Heuzey carried out excavations in the palace at Vergina. These were resumed in 1937 by C. Romaios and were continued subsequently (1952-1963) by M. Andronikos.

In 1968 the British archaeologist N. Hammond proposed the theory that ancient Aigai should be sought at Vergina, and not at

Silver cinerary hydria with gold wreath from the Prince's Tomb

Painted stele from the cemetery at Vergina

Edessa as was formerly believed. Truly, in 1978 Manolis Andronikos brought to light at Vergina the famous royal tombs.

As visitors walk through the archaeological site, along the two-kilometre road linking the village of Vergina with Palatitsia, they behold the Tumulus Cemetery, a large expanse scattered with burial mounds or tumuli.

Most of them are family tumuli, about one metre high and 15-20 metres in diameter, dating from the Protogeometric period (c. 1000 BC) into Hellenistic times (3rd c. BC). The dead were buried either in pits or in large jars, and two vases containing offerings were usually placed alongside them.

The most impressive of the built tombs is the so-called Romaios Tomb, which is about 500 metres north of the palace and is dated to the third century BC. On its façade are four engaged Ionic columns and a pediment, while the marble double door is decorated with relief nails, in imitation of a wooden portal. The interior of the tomb holds an elegant marble throne, on the arms of which rest two small sphinxes.

In 1977-1978, Manolis Andronikos brought to light at Vergina the Royal Tombs, which were covered by a manmade mound, the "Megali Toumba" or

Façade of the tomb of Philip II

Great Tumulus. The largest tomb was uncovered first, which according to the excavator belonged to Philip II, who was assassinated by his bodyguard Pausanias in the theatre of Aigai.

This is a built tomb with antechamber and main chamber connected by a marble door, either side of which two engaged Doric columns and two antae support the epistyle with triglyphs and metopes, on which the painted decoration is preserved. Above the cornice is an Ionic frieze, painted with a hunting scene in which Philip and his son Alexander are perhaps protagonists. In the burial chamber stood the marble sarcophagus, inside which was the gold larnax containing the cremated bones of Philip, wrapped in purple cloth. Deposited upon the bones was a precious gold wreath consisting of 313 oak leaves and 68 acorns. Embossed on the lid of the larnax is the solar emblem of the Macedonian kings.

Many other precious grave goods were found in the same chamber, including the remains of a wooden couch with ivory adornments. The antechamber contained a marble sarcophagus with a smaller gold larnax inside, the remains in which were perhaps of Kleopatra, the seventh and last wife of Philip. Her bones were wrapped in purple and gold cloth, and placed beside them was an exquisite gold diadem, a masterpiece in the minor arts. Next to the sarcophagus was a gold myrtle wreath consisting of 80 leaves and 113 flowers, as well as other grave goods belonging to the king, among them two gilded bronze greaves and a gold gorytos or quiver-bowcase.

A smaller tomb in the tumulus belongs to a young prince, whom some scholars identify as Alexander IV, son of Alexander the Great. The Prince's Tomb has an austere Doric façade with two antae and two marble jambs supporting the lintel. Around the antechamber was a narrow frieze with scenes of chariot race. A built table with circular depression in the middle was the base for the silver cinerary hydria, containing the bones of the deceased. Placed on the vase was a gold oak wreath. The finds in the chamber included a host of silver vases and vessels, a large silvered iron lamp-stand, small ivory reliefs, and so on. The so-called Tomb of Persephone, a quadrilateral poros building, was found looted. The subjects of the wall-paintings in its interior relate to the Underworld.

The original form of the tumulus that covered the royal tombs at Vergina has been reconstructed as a shelter, which visitors enter to enjoy the architectural monuments and the splendid artifacts.

The Palace of Aigai is built in a superb location with a view over the plain of the River Haliakmon. At its centre is a square court surrounded by four porticoes with Doric columns, 16 on each side. The monumental entrance is on the east side and is articulated in three successive spaces.

South of the entrance is a circular room which, according to an inscription found there, was dedicated to Herakles. At the centre of the south side there was a large space open onto the court. These two chambers were reception and symposium halls. Preserved in the hall west of the entrance is a wonderful mosaic pavement with a vegetal composition at the centre and a female figure in each corner.

On the west side are three ancillary rooms and three large square rooms. The north side is badly damaged. Nonetheless, it seems that a veranda extended along its length, offering an excellent view of the vast Macedonian plain.

The Theatre of Aigai lies a short distance to the north of the palace. The cavea is divided into nine cunei. Only the front row of seats has survived, which were of stone, whereas the rest were of wood. Part of the foundations of the skene and the stone of the thymele, at the centre of the orchestra, have also been revealed.

Some 80 metres north of the theatre are the foundations of the small temple of Eukleia, with pronaos and cella, which is dated to the second half of the fourth century BC. "Eukleia", which means glory, good repute, was an epithet of Artemis, who was worshipped also as an independent deity in many parts of Greece. Further east of this sanctuary, the sanctuary of the Mother of the Gods is being excavated.

Gold larnax from the tomb of Philip II

PELLA

For strategic reasons, King Archelaos I (413-399 BC), son of Perdikkas II, transferred the capital of the Macedonian State from Aigai to Pella. He fortified the hitherto insignificant city, organized the army and the navy, reformed the administration and maintained excellent relations with the Greek cities in the South. He spent lavishly on organizing and adorning the new capital, as well as on constructing his magnificent palace, which was decorated with murals by the greatest painter of the age, Zeuxis.

Pella reached its zenith in the reign of Philip II (360-336 BC), while with the conquests of Alexander the Great (336-323 BC) its glory radiated to the ends of the then-known world.

Pella continued to be a political and cultural centre of Greece until the second century BC, despite the endless conflicts between the successors (Diadochoi) to Alexander. In 168 BC, the last King of Macedonia, Perseus, was defeated at the battle of Pydna, by the Roman general Aemilius Paulus, who stripped the capital of its art treasures and monuments, in order to celebrate his triumph in Rome.

The city was later reconstituted as a Roman provincial town, Colonia Julia Augusta Pella, while Thessalonike was named capital of the province. In the early first century BC, Pella was destroyed totally, most probably by an earthquake.

In the south part of the city, large luxurious residences were brought to light, built in insulae, in accordance with the Hippodamean system, thus named after its creator, Hippodamos from Miletos, philosopher, architect and urban-planner of the fifth century BC. These private houses range in area from 1,000 to 2,300 square metres and belonged to officials and wealthy Macedonians.

The living quarters were built around a central peristyle court, source of illumination and ventilation for the house. In many cases, parts of the staircases leading to the upper storey are preserved.

In the so-called House of Dionysos, some of the Ionic columns have been restored in the peristyle of the north sector, where the family apartments were located. The south sector was larger and also had a court, around which were the symposium and reception halls. All the floors were decorated with mosaics, executed in river pebbles and gravel.

The mosaics now exhibited in the museum come from this house. Dated around 300 BC, they include representations of Dionysos mounted on a panther, of Centaurs, of a griffin attacking a deer, and of a lion hunt.

The second large mansion is that of the Rape of Helen, with the corresponding subject on the main mosaic floor. Represented on the second mosaic is a deer

View of the wealthy houses of Pella

hunt, which is signed by the artist Gnosis. The mosaic with scene of Amazonomachy is rather ineptly executed.

To the north of the area of private houses lie the ruins of the ancient agora, covering an area of 70,000 square metres. At the centre is a large square, surrounded by stoas, numerous shops and workshops, while on the south side of the agora were public buildings.

A short distance to the east of the agora, cemeteries of various periods, from the fifth century BC to Roman times, have been excavated.

Important too are the sanctuaries of Aphrodite and of the Mother of the Gods, to the north of the agora. On the middle one of the three hills rising to the north are the ruins of the palace of the Macedonian kings, occupying an area of approximately 60,000 square metres.

The mosaic of a stag hunt by Gnosis

THESSALONIKE

In 315 BC, King Kassander of Macedonia (350-297 BC), son of Antipater, a general of Alexander the Great, founded the city of Thessalonike at the innermost reach of the Thermaic Gulf, in an area where there is evidence of continuous habitation from the sixth millennium BC. As the ancient geographer Strabo records, populations from 26 settlements in the surrounding region gathered in the new city, which Kassander named after his wife, Thessalonike. After the battle of Pydna, in 168 BC, Macedonia became a Roman province and in 147 BC Thessalonike was declared its capital.

Cicero was exiled to the city in 58 BC, while Pompey sought refuge there in 49 BC, to escape Julius Caesar. Thessalonike was visited twice by Paul the Apostle, in AD 50 and 56. In the late third century AD, the Roman Tetrarch Galerius Maximianus made Thessalonike his seat and in 305 BC constructed an impressive palatial complex in its eastern sector. In the same period, Demetrios was martyred here. He became the city's patron saint, to whom the renowned majestic five-aisled basilica in the centre is dedicated.

In the fourth century AD, Emperor Constantine founded Constantinople as new capital of the Eastern Roman Empire, but also constructed a new harbour and reinforced the walls of Thessalonike. In the fifth century AD, Emperor Theodosios ordered his general Ormisdas to circumvallate the city with even stronger fortifications, large sections of which still stand today. Capital of the Byzantine Empire was Constantinople and co-regnant city was Thessalonike, from where Cyril and Methodius set out in the ninth century AD to convert the Slavs to Christianity.

The Rotunda, a building of circular plan (diam. 24.15 m.), is roofed by a large dome and has walls 6 metres thick. It seems to have been initially a pagan temple, dedicated to the emperor or to other gods, like the Pantheon in Rome. In the late fourth century BC it was converted into a Christian church, in the sixteenth century into a Muslim mosque. After the liberation of Thessaloniki (1912), it became a church once more, and subsequently a museum.

South of the Rotunda is the so-called Kamara, the Arch of Galerius, which comprises two pillars united by an arch. What we see today is just one part of a four-pillar monument, which the Thessalonikans erected in AD 303 to honour Galerius after his victorious campaign against the Persians.

The splendid palace of Galerius, remains of which are visible in Navarinou Square, was adorned with mosaic floors. The apartments for members of the royal family were arranged around a square atrium, while the large spaces around the central building were reception and banqueting halls. The octagonal building on the

View of the Byzantine walls

The Derveni krater

southwest side of the court, lavishly decorated with reliefs, was most probably the throne room.

The name of Hippodrome Square echoes the fact that buried beneath the modern buildings are the ruins of the hippodrome, east of the palace.

The ancient agora of Thessalonike was built in the second century AD and consists of a paved piazza (146 x 97 m.) surrounded on three sides by series of rooms and a small theatre on the east side. Taking advantage of the sloping ground, a second, subterranean vaulted stoa (cryptoporticus) was constructed on the south side, possibly to serve as a public storeroom.

Even further south is the commercial sector, with many shops. The agora was abandoned in the fifth century AD, as administrative services were concentrated in the palace.

Reconstruction of the agora of Thessalonike →

D elos, a barren islet in the Aegean, developed from early times into a commercial habour, thanks to its geographical location at the centre of the Cyclades. In Antiquity it was an important port of call on the maritime trade routes between Syria, Egypt, the Euxine Pontus (Black Sea), Greece and Italy. Tradition has it that the island's first inhabitants, in the third millennium BC, were Carians and Lelegians. Life continued without interruption into Mycenaean and Geometric times, when Delos became a major panhellenic religious centre, as famed as Olympia and Delphi.

According to myth, it was the birthplace of Apollo and his twin sister Artemis. The Titaness Leto was said to have searched for somewhere to bring her children, sired by Zeus, into the world. But no mountain, city or island would receive her, because they feared the wrath of Hera. The only place that accepted her was the tiny island floating invisible (a-delos) between the waves. Then Poseidon fixed it to the seabed and brought it up to the surface, making it visible, i.e. delos, the place of Leto's accouchement.

The island enjoyed a particular heyday in the Archaic period (7th-6th c. BC). Delos is mentioned in Homer's Odyssey as the Ionians' common place of worship. In the sixth century BC, the Athenian tyrant Peisistratos built the Archaic temple of Apollo and removed all the graves from around it, thus purifying the isle from pollution of death and inaugurating Athenian influence over it.

After the Persian Wars, Delos became seat of the Athenian League. Initially, the treasury of contributions from the allied cities was kept there, although this was soon transferred to the Athenian Acropolis. In 426 BC the second purification of the island took place and all births and deaths there were forbidden. In addition to the old annual festival of the "Delia", a new festival was then instituted, even more splendid and celebrated every five years.

Delos flourished and prospered anew in the Hellenistic period, when on the initiative of Antigonos Gonatas it was declared independent and became the religious centre of the Koinon of Islanders. When the Romans vanquished the Macedonians at Pydna (168 BC), the island returned again to Athenian domination, but under Roman control. There was a remarkable influx of foreigners, mainly merchants and bankers from all neighbouring Mediterranean lands, who settled on Delos and transformed it into a thriving cosmopolitan commercial centre.

However, in 88 and 69 BC, when Mithridates Eupator, King of Pontos, waged war on the Romans, the Delians sided with the latter and Mithridates' Parthians savagely

Herme's Residence

The Naxian lions on Delos

destroyed and plundered the island. With this devastation decline set in and by the second century AD the sole inhabitants of Delos were the custodians of the sanctuary.

The harbour where today's visitors come ashore is in the position of the ancient one. Hereabouts was the commercial sector with the agora of the Competaliasts or Hermaists, which were associations of merchants from Italy, the Stoa of Philip V, the South Stoa built by the kings of Pergamon in the third century BC, the agora of the Delians, the shops and numerous statues.

The steps of the propylaia, built by the Athenians in the second century BC, lead into the sanctuary of Apollo, where there was a host of monuments, temples, covered stoas, altars and five small "treasuries", similar to the treasuries at Olympia and Delphi. Here too was the Oikos of the Naxians, of the seventh century BC, on the north wall of which the Naxians had erected a colossal Archaic statue of Apollo.

The three temples of Apollo were built by the Athenians; the poros temple in the sixth   century BC, the marble one in the fifth century BC, and the temple of the Delians, the only one that was peripteral with 6 x 13 Doric columns. Construction of the last temple was continued by the Delians in the fourth century BC, but it was never completed.

Here too stood the bouleuterion and the prytaneion, as well as the Keraton, that is the altar of horns, around which Theseus is believed to have danced when he stopped at Delos on his return voyage from Crete. The northwest part of the sanctuary was dedicated to Artemis.

On the left side of the road leading from the sanctuary to the Sacred Lake are the

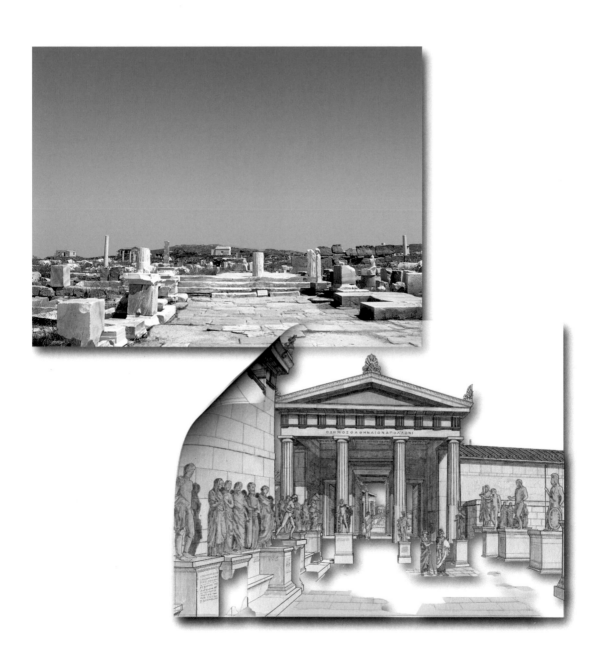

Reconstruction of the propylaia of the temple of Apollo →

ΟΔΗΜΟΣΟ

ΑΙΩΝΑΠΟΛΛΩΝΙ

Hypostyle Hall, of uncertain purpose, and the ruins of the Dodecatheon. On the right is the sixth-century BC temple of Apollo's mother, Leto, and behind this is the large second-century BC agora of the Italians.

Opposite the agora is a terrace on which the Naxians set up a row of lions, in the seventh century BC. Five of these statues survive (the originals have been moved to the museum and replaced by replicas on the site), while in the seventeenth century a sixth lion, now headless, was taken by Francesco Morosini to Venice, where it stands in the Arsenale. The Sacred Lake, where Apollo was born under a palm tree, has been drained and a wall built around its perimeter.

Another road commences at the harbour and leads to the Theatre Quarter, which is of considerable interest for the study of private houses of the Hellenistic period (2nd-1st c. BC). All have a central court that provided light and air to the residential apartments developed around it. The larger houses have two or more storeys and many are decorated with wall-paintings and mosaic floors, such as the so-called Dionysos House, with the mosaic of Dionysos upon a panther, the house of the trident, the house of Dioskourides and Kleopatra, with statues of the owners, and others.

The theatre, built in the third century BC, has a circular orchestra, a skene and proscenium, and a cavea accommodating 5,500 spectators. In front of it are the ruins of a large cistern for collecting rainwater. Beyond the theatre, on the slopes of Mount Kynthos, are the largest water cistern on Delos and houses with tessellated pavements, such as the house of the dolphins and the house of the masks, as well as sanctuaries dedicated to Syrian and Egyptian deities.

Reconstruction of the Sacred Way →

CRETE

C rete was the cradle of the oldest civilization in Europe, which was named Minoan after the legendary king Minos. Myth has it that Poseidon offered Minos, son of Zeus and Europa, the kingdom of Crete, but that Minos, instead of sacrificing to his benefactor a sacred white bull that leapt from the waves, kept it for himself and sacrificed an animal from his herd.

The god punished Minos by arousing in his wife, Queen Pasiphae, an erotic passion for the bull. From their union was born the Minotaur, a monster with bull's head and human body, which Minos imprisoned in the Labyrinth. The Athenians, who had slain Minos' son Androgeus, were obliged to send every nine years a blood tribute to Crete of seven boys and seven girls, which the monster devoured. The Prince of Athens, Theseus, slew the Minotaur and managed to come out of the Labyrinth, thanks to the help of Minos' daughter Ariadne.

Archaeological investigations have shown that human presence on Crete goes back to the Neolithic Age (6000-2800 BC). During the Early Minoan period (2800-2000 BC) the island's inhabitants lived in settlements, in houses frequently with painted walls and paved courtyards. Trade and seafaring flourished.

The beginning of the great heyday of Minoan Civilization is marked by the appearance of the palaces, in the Middle Minoan period (2000-1600 BC), which were foci of religious, political and economic authority. Five palaces have been brought to light so far, at Knossos, Phaistos, Archanes, Zakros and Malia, although there are indications of the existence of others.

Around 1700 BC, a great earthquake destroyed the palaces, but these were rebuilt in the Late Minoan period (1650-1400 BC), even more resplendent and with technical improvements. They were decorated with superb wall-paintings which are an invaluable source of information on Minoan life.

During the Postpalatial or Mycenaean period (1450-1100 BC), the Achaeans invaded Crete and installed the Achaean dynasty in the palace of Knossos. They organized a complex bureaucratic system and introduced many Mycenaean elements in architecture and art.

In the ensuing centuries, down to 69 BC, when the island was captured by the Romans, Crete never lost its importance, since it lies at the crossroad of cultures and communications of Mediterranean peoples.

Wall-painting of the prince with the lilies

KNOSSOS

Stone libation vessel in the form of a bull's head, from Knossos

At the height of its glory, Knossos is estimated to have had several thousand inhabitants. The so-called palace of Minos occupies an area of 20,000 square metres and was the administrative, religious and economic centre of the country. Symbol of royal power was the double axe, the "labrys", and the palace of the labrys was named the Labyrinth.

Excavations at Knossos, which were begun in 1878 by Minos Kalokairinos and were continued in 1900 by the British archaeologist Sir Arthur Evans, brought to light the traces of a palace that had been built around 1900 BC and destroyed by earthquake around 1600 BC. A second, larger palace was built upon its ruins, but this too was destroyed completely in 1450 BC. Some spaces were reused from 1400 to 1380 BC, after which they were abandoned.

The palace was at least three-storeyed and its entire weight was supported by the columns and the architraves. The columns were of timber and some were fluted or ribbed. They tapered from the capital to the base, a characteristic feature of Minoan and subsequently of Mycenaean architecture. The walls were covered with a layer of plaster and straw, and a final coat of fine lime plaster on which various representations were painted.

On each side of the palace is an entrance leading into the central court, around which the apartments of the complex are ranged. On the west side is a second paved court, to which the main entrance to the palace leads. In the court are three large pits, which were probably sacral repositories into which redundant cult paraphernalia was thrown, as well as two altars. The propylon, with a central column, was roofed and leads to the corridor of the procession, thus named after the wall-painting of the procession of some 500 adorants that decorated its walls.

The corridor to the south leads to the hypostyle staircase that was the

Reconstruction of the north entrance to the palace of Knossos →

Storage jar (pithos) from the palace magazines

entrance to the old palace. Adjacent to it was a hostel, which Evans named the Caravanserai.

The south gate of the palace leads to the corridors that end at the central court. Close to the west corridor, the wall-painting of the Prince with the Lilies was found.

The processional causeway leads to the south propylaia, from where a grand staircase goes up to the three-column shrine, the roof of which rested on three columns and three pillars. The rectangular space right of the staircase was called a Mycenaean megaron or a Greek temple, possibly dedicated to Rhea. A doorway opens into the treasury, in which cult vessels were found.

A corridor passes to the west of the sanctuary and into the so-called great hall and the shrine, with the famous wall-painting dubbed "La Parisienne".

On the ground floor is a suite of 18 long narrow magazines in which 150 large storage jars (pithoi) were placed. There were also crypts, as well as the throne room and its antechamber. On the north wall of the main room is the gypsum throne, and around the walls are gypsum benches. Griffins were painted on the wall and opposite these is a lustral basin.

Next to the throne room is a staircase to the upper storey. Exhibited in the room directly above the throne room are replicas of wall-paintings found in the palace (the originals are in the Herakleion Museum). Adjacent to the staircase is the tripartite shrine, the form of which is known from miniature frescoes.

To the south is the antechamber of the pillar crypts, a hypostyle hall with cisterns in which libations were made on the pillars, that is sacred stones inscribed with the double axe and representing deities.

In part of the east wing of the palace the architect was able to construct a four-storey edifice. A spectacular staircase with gypsum treads and parapets, and a corridor, lead into the king's or the hall of the double axes. There stood the king's throne and to the east, between two pier-and-door partitions (polythyra), was the audience chamber. The south door opened into a corridor leading to the queen's megaron, where superb wall-paintings, such as that of the dolphins, were found. To the west is the queen's bathroom, with the bathtub and the "boudoir", after which is a lightwell and a small lavatory.

Other interesting quarters in the same wing are the shrine of the double axe, the house of the sacrificed bulls, the house of the sacred bema, the stonecutter's workshop, the potter's workshop, the magazine of the giant pithoi, the corridor of the gaming board, and so on.

A corridor from the central court leads to the north wing of the palace and to the large hypostyle hall known as the customs house, because this was the terminus of the road from the two harbours of Knossos.

A prepalatial complex with curved corners, northwest of the court, was called by Evans the "dungeon". Further west is the lustral basin, in which foreign visitors took their purificatory ablutions. From the north gate a processional causeway continues outside the palace to the theatral area, with seating in L-shaped arrangement for 500 persons.

Part of the interior of the palace of Knossos

RHODES

The ancient Greeks believed that at the moment Rhodos, daughter of Poseidon, leapt up from the sea, the Sun-god Helios beheld her, as he was making his daily journey round earth. Dazzled by her beauty, he chose her as his portion when the gods shared out the world between them.

According to tradition, the island's first inhabitants were the daemonic craftsmen, the Telchines, who had come there from Minoan Crete. However, archaeological investigations have shown that Rhodes was settled already from the Neo-lithic Age. The Telchines were followed by Achaeans from the Argolid, after which came Dorians from Tiryns - so is the tradition - led by the son of Herakles, Tlepolemos, who became King of Rhodes.

Around 700 BC, the island's three major cities - Lindos, Kamiros and Ialysos - founded the so-called "Dorian Hexapolis", an alliance that included Kos, Knidos and Halikarnassos. Centre of the hexapolis was the temple of Apollo Tri-opios in Knidos, where annual games were held in honour of the god.

At the end of the Peloponnesian War (431-404 BC), the three ancient cities of Lindos, Kamiros and Ialysos united in founding the city of Rhodes at the north tip of the island, and established it as their common political and administrative centre. The new city was fortified with strong walls, which proved able to withstand the one-year-long siege of Demetrios Poliorketes (305-304 BC), who wanted to force Rhodes to take part in the war he had declared against Ptolemy of Egypt.

The campaign ended in compromise, with terms that guaranteed Rhodes her independence. To commemorate this event, the Lindian bronze-sculptor Chares, pupil of Lysippos, created the Colossus, a 32-metre high statue of the god Helios, one of the Seven Wonders of the ancient world. The position of the statue astride the harbour entrance, so that ships entering port sailed under its open legs, has been disputed. It seems more likely that it stood on the site where the Grand Master's palace was later built. The Colossus was toppled by earthquake in 227/6 BC and hundreds of years later, in the seventh century AD, was taken to pieces and sold to the Saracens.

The ancient city of Rhodes was built in 408 BC and designed by the great urban-planner, Hippodamos of Miletos; the modern city follows in greater part the ancient grid. The acropolis was on San Stefano hill (Monte Smith), where ruins of the temple of Zeus Polieus still stand.

A short distance away is the Hellenistic temple of Apollo Pythios, which has been partially restored on its northeast side. Close to the temple are the ruins

Entrance to the Castello, where the sanctuary of Helios is located

of the stadium, the gymnasium and the odeum, which in all probability housed the renowned school of rhetoric where, among others, Cicero and Julius Caesar studied.

The hills around Kamiros are scattered with ancient cemeteries. On the acropolis stood the Hellenistic temple of Athena Polias, of which only scant remnants are visible. The foundations of a large stoa, 200 metres long, in the Doric order have also been found.

A Hellenistic temple of Athena Polias also existed at Ialysos, 10 kilometres west of Rhodes, on Mount Philerimos.

It was in the Doric order and amphiprostyle, with six columns front and back. On the south slope of the acropolis are the ruins of a monumental fountain with four marble lion-head waterspouts.

The city of Lindos was built on a rocky promontory on the east coast of the island. On the highest point (116 m. a.s.l.) is the acropolis, which is surrounded by the Medieval castle built by the Knights of St John of Jerusalem, who were based on Rhodes. The role of the spacious Doric stoa, 88 metres long, which visitors first behold, was decorative and enhanced the sanctuary of Athena (2nd c. BC) situated behind it. Beyond is a monumental staircase of 34 steps, built in the fourth century BC, which

Characteristic detail from the entrance to the harbour of Rhodes

Reconstruction of the temple of Apollo Pythios →

The Laocoon group, a Rhodian sculpture

leads to the propylaia, the form of which was influenced by that of the Propylaia on the Athenian Acropolis.

The temple of Athena Lindia was built in the sixth century BC by Kleobolos, one of the Seven Sages of Antiquity, who was tyrant of Lindos for forty years. In 342 BC the temple was destroyed by fire, but was rebuilt immediately.

The new temple, in the Doric order and amphiprostyle, with four columns on front and back, comprised a pronaos, cella and opisthodomos. It housed the chryselephantine statue of the goddess, whose left hand rested on the shield, while the right one held a bowl (phiale).

TEMPLES

T emples are the most important buildings in ancient Greek architecture. Their size and type vary, but their entrance normally faces east.

The plainest and smallest type is the temple in antis (I). The prostyle (II) is also of simple type, whereas the amphiprostyle (III) is more complex, with columns on front and back. The peripteral temple (IV) is the most representative type, characterized by the colonnade known as the pteron (2), which surrounds the central part, the cella (5). The pronaos (3) is in front of the cella and may be in antis (IV), which means that it has columns between pillars (8), or prostyle (V). The opisthodomos (4) has a similar form. The cella, which worshippers were not allowed to enter, housed the cult statue (6), which was usually framed by an internal colonnade, often two-storeyed (7). The double pteron around the perimeter is typical of the dipteral temple (V).

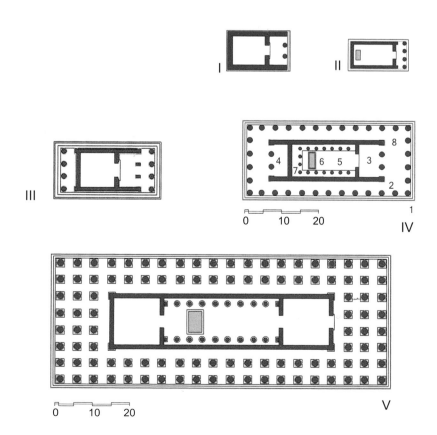

ARCHITECTURAL ORDERS

T he architectural orders are: Doric (D), Ionic (I) and Corinthian (C). They were applied not only to temples but also to public and private buildings.

The Doric order is simpler, since it transfers to stone the earlier morphology of wooden constructions. The columns, which usually have fluted shafts (13), stand on the stylobate (12), the highest level of the usually three-stepped crepis (10).

The Ionic order has more slender columns, set on a base (23) and with fluted shaft ending in a taenia. Typical is the capital (I-14) with large volutes.

The Corinthian order, also slender, was applied later and is distinguished by its column capital (C-14) with small volutes and acanthus leaves.

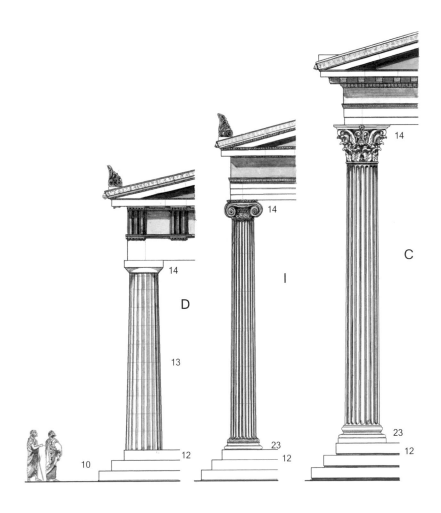